FEED ME
NOW!

Bill Granger

FEED ME NOW!

PHOTOGRAPHS BY John Kernick

Quadrille
PUBLISHING

contents

notes

All spoon measures are level unless otherwise stated:
1 teaspoon = 5ml spoon; 1 tablespoon = 15ml spoon.

Use fresh herbs, sea salt and freshly ground black pepper unless
otherwise specified. Where white pepper is suggested, black pepper will
be a suitable alternative.

Use organic or free-range eggs. Anyone who is pregnant or in a
vulnerable health group should avoid recipes using raw egg whites or
lightly cooked eggs.

Suggested cooking times relate to conventional ovens. If you are using
a fan-assisted oven, it is advisable to set the oven temperature 15–20°C
lower, or 1 Gas Mark lower for a fan-assisted gas oven. However, for
baking cakes and biscuits, I recommend conventional rather than
fan-assisted cooking.

I really don't think we can underestimate the importance of good food in our lives. Providing nutritious and delicious meals for loved ones – and taking time out to eat together – is one of life's prime sources of satisfaction. It is also fundamental to good health and happiness. But, in today's world, where the pace of life seems to be ever increasing, and we are all juggling competing priorities, time for preparing and sharing meals can easily be compromised. But it needn't be… nor should it be.

I wrote the recipes for *Feed Me Now!* to help resolve my own family-work life balance. And also as a response to people telling me about their meal dilemmas, which I pondered and considered in relation to my own. The book is full of different quick meal solutions – from breakfast through to dinner – for day-to-day modern life. Whether it's a hastily prepared lunch from leftovers, a speedy midweek meal, a quick sweet treat, or effortless entertaining you are looking for, you'll find plenty of ideas here. I've also included a variety of slow-cooked meals that you can prepare ahead with ease.

Food is complex. It feeds so many of our needs – emotional, social and purely physical. On a basic level it is fuel, and at the other end of the spectrum it is pure indulgence and pleasure. Food just for fuel can be heartless, soulless and uninspiring, yet food just for pleasure, while offering instant gratification, gives no long-term sustenance on any level. I like to provide food for family and friends to satisfy all needs.

When I do get a meal on the table, everything does stop and we do talk and enjoy each other… and escape. A rainy Saturday, sitting down to a surprise pasta lunch, some seasonal greens, simply dressed, and an unusual daytime glass of wine, reminds me what life is all about.

I feel strongly that mealtimes should not be rushed. Food shared with loved ones – with time to savour the company as well as the tastes and textures – makes you feel whole, satisfied, content, invigorated and revitalised. I try to achieve this daily, to share food prepared with love… well, most of the time anyway, and sometimes quickly! I truly believe it is my family's lifeblood.

I sincerely hope that the uncomplicated recipes in *Feed Me Now!* will give you fresh inspiration in the kitchen. However busy you are, please make mealtimes with your family and friends a priority – and enjoy the simple magic that sharing a beautiful meal can bring.

rise & shine

Simple breakfasts in our house might be quick bowls of muesli, yoghurt and berries, or slightly more lavish but equally easy plates of mozzarella, basil leaves, tomato and prosciutto, with fresh bread or toast on the side. Other days call for a little more variety – decadent, rich and crisp toasted muesli, platters of fresh fruit and the best creamy yoghurt, plus toasted pre-made breakfast loaves, or perhaps freshly baked muffins – the ingredients weighed out the night before in readiness for quick morning baking. These are the breakfasts that feed my family during the week, and the chorus of delight from them gives my day a special start and puts a spring in my step. But of course it's those lazy weekends, when the deadline for breakfast is a luxurious two hours later, that I enjoy the most. The sheer thrill a simple session of cooking gives my children, not to mention the little carb injection if we go for oaty hotcakes with caramel bananas, keeps us motoring through the day.

16 servings (as a sprinkle)
125g unsalted butter
60g soft brown sugar
2 teaspoons ground cinnamon
300g rolled oats
160g almonds (with skin), roughly
  chopped

to serve
yoghurt and/or poached fruit

"Far too rich to have on its own, I use this muesli more as a crunchy textural sprinkle over yoghurt and poached fruit – either for breakfast or as an afternoon snack for the kids."

cinnamon crunch muesli

Preheat the oven to 160°C/Gas 3. Line a large baking tray with baking paper. Place the butter, sugar and cinnamon in a large pan over a medium heat. Stir until the butter has melted and the sugar dissolved. Turn off the heat, add the oats and almonds and stir to coat evenly.

Spread the mixture evenly on the prepared tray. Bake for about 30 minutes, stirring occasionally, until lightly browned. Allow to cool completely before storing in an airtight container.

serves 4

350g rhubarb, chopped into 5cm lengths
500g strawberries, hulled and halved
1 tablespoon plain flour
50g caster sugar

topping

120g untoasted muesli
25g plain flour
55g caster sugar
100g cold butter, cut into small pieces

to serve

thick Greek yoghurt

"For the topping, you can also use cinnamon crunch muesli (see page 10) before it is toasted."

rhubarb & strawberry breakfast crisp

Preheat the oven to 200°C/Gas 6. Place the chopped rhubarb and strawberries in a baking dish. Sprinkle with the flour and sugar and toss to combine. Bake for 10 minutes.

For the topping, mix the muesli, flour and sugar together in a large bowl, add the butter and rub in with your fingertips until the mixture resembles coarse breadcrumbs.

Sprinkle the topping over the fruit mixture and bake for 30 minutes until golden brown and bubbling. Serve with thick Greek yoghurt.

serves 4

hotcakes

185g plain flour

1½ teaspoons baking powder

¼ teaspoon ground cinnamon

good pinch of freshly grated nutmeg (optional)

pinch of sea salt

1 tablespoon caster sugar

25g rolled oats

375ml buttermilk

1 medium egg, lightly beaten

35g butter, melted, plus extra to grease pan

to serve

caramel bananas or blueberry maple syrup
  (see right), or raspberries sprinkled with
  icing sugar and lightly crushed

(illustrated on previous pages)

oaty hotcakes
with fruit toppings

To make the hotcake batter, sift the flour, baking powder, cinnamon, nutmeg and salt together into a bowl. Stir the sugar and oats through, then make a well in the centre. Pour in the buttermilk and egg, stirring until just mixed. Add the melted butter and stir to combine. Set aside.

To cook the hotcakes, heat a large non-stick frying pan over a medium heat and brush a little butter over the base. Pour in 2 or 3 small ladlefuls of batter, being careful not to overcrowd the pan, and cook for 2–3 minutes, until bubbles appear on the surface. Turn and cook for a further 2–3 minutes. Transfer to a plate and keep warm while cooking the rest.

Serve the hotcakes with the caramel bananas, blueberry maple syrup or lightly crushed raspberries.

"Two toppings for these wholesome hotcakes – caramel bananas for when the windows are frosty and misted, and berries for days when the sun is shining."

caramel bananas

3 bananas
60g butter
90g soft brown sugar
½ teaspoon natural vanilla extract

Halve the bananas lengthways and cut each piece in three. Put the butter, sugar, vanilla and 2 tablespoons water in a large frying pan over a medium heat and cook until the mixture forms a caramel and darkens. Add the bananas and toss through until well coated.

blueberry maple syrup

125g blueberries, fresh or frozen
250ml maple syrup

Place the blueberries and maple syrup in a small saucepan over a medium heat. Bring to the boil, then reduce the heat to low and simmer for 10 minutes, until slightly reduced.

makes 2 loaves; each 12 slices

45g soft light brown sugar

30g almonds, chopped

255ml soured cream

1 teaspoon bicarbonate of soda

100g unsalted butter, melted

230g caster sugar

2 medium eggs, lightly beaten

250g plain flour

1 teaspoon baking powder

1 teaspoon ground cinnamon

250g mashed ripe banana (about
  2 medium bananas)

melt & mix
banana bread

Preheat the oven to 180°C/Gas 4. Grease and line two 10 x 18cm loaf tins with baking paper. In a bowl, mix together the brown sugar and almonds and set aside.

In a large bowl, mix together the soured cream and bicarbonate of soda, leave to stand for 5 minutes, then stir in the melted butter, caster sugar and eggs. Sift the flour, baking powder and cinnamon into another bowl. Gradually fold in the soured cream mixture, followed by the mashed bananas.

Divide the mixture equally between the prepared tins and sprinkle the brown sugar mixture on top. Bake for 1–1¼ hours or until a skewer inserted into the centre of each loaf comes out clean. Set aside to cool in the tins for about 20 minutes, then turn out onto a wire rack to cool completely.

"No banana bread recipe ever uses enough of those blackened bananas sitting in the fruit bowl, so bake more than one loaf and freeze pre-sliced – ready for morning toasting or breakfast-on-the-run."

makes 12

250g plain flour

2 teaspoons baking powder

1 teaspoon ground cinnamon

95g soft light brown sugar

80ml buttermilk

2 medium eggs, lightly beaten

1 teaspoon natural vanilla extract

80g unsalted butter, melted

330g mashed steamed pumpkin or butternut
  squash (about 360g uncooked weight)

70g sultanas

pumpkin & cinnamon muffins

Preheat the oven to 190°C/Gas 5. Line a 12-hole, 125ml capacity muffin tin with muffin paper cases.

Sift the flour, baking powder and cinnamon into a large mixing bowl. Stir through the brown sugar.

Combine the buttermilk, eggs, vanilla extract and melted butter in a large bowl. Add to the dry ingredients and stir until just combined. Stir through the mashed pumpkin and sultanas.

Divide the mixture evenly between the muffin cases and bake for 20 minutes or until golden and a fine skewer inserted into the centre comes out clean. Remove the muffins and set aside to cool slightly before serving.

serves 4

1 tablespoon extra virgin olive oil

1 onion, finely chopped

2 garlic cloves, crushed

1 teaspoon ground cumin

400g tin chopped tomatoes

2 teaspoons brown sugar

2 x 400g tins red kidney beans, rinsed

sea salt

freshly ground black pepper

juice of 1 lime, or to taste

handful coriander leaves

1 green chilli, deseeded and finely chopped

100g feta cheese, crumbled

3 spring onions, thinly sliced

spicy beans
with feta

Preheat the oven to 160°C/Gas 3. Heat the olive oil in a large flameproof casserole over a medium heat. Add the onion and cook, stirring, for 5–6 minutes until soft. Add the garlic and cumin and cook, stirring, for another minute.

Add the tomatoes, sugar and 125ml water. Bring to the boil, then reduce the heat and simmer for 10 minutes. Stir in the kidney beans and season with salt and pepper. Put the lid on the casserole and bake in the oven for 30 minutes.

Just before serving, add lime juice to taste and scatter over the coriander, chilli, feta and spring onions.

"As an alternative to toast, try these beans with corn tortillas. Wrap a stack in foil and pop in the oven 5 minutes before the beans will be ready."

serves 2

125g cherry tomatoes

2 teaspoons lime juice

¼ teaspoon sugar

1 tablespoon shredded coriander leaves

sea salt

freshly ground black pepper

1 Spanish chorizo sausage, about 120g, diced

2 spring onions, sliced

2 medium eggs, lightly beaten

2 bread rolls

grab-and-go
breakfast.
sandwich

Halve the cherry tomatoes and place in a bowl with the lime juice, sugar, shredded coriander, salt and pepper. Stir gently to combine.

Place a frying pan over a medium heat. When hot, add the chorizo and fry until lightly browned. Add the spring onions and stir for 30 seconds until softened. Pour over the beaten eggs. When they start to set around the edge of the pan, gently stir and turn the mixture with a spatula or wooden spoon until the eggs are just set.

Break open the bread rolls, divide the chorizo and scrambled eggs between them and serve with the tomato salad.

"For an alternate all-in-one version, blister the cherry tomatoes in the pan after the chorizo has been cooking for a couple of minutes, and finish the lot with shredded coriander."

serves 4

4 slices ciabatta or sourdough bread

4 tablespoons extra virgin olive oil

sea salt

pinch of dried red chilli flakes

8 medium eggs

2 small heads of radicchio or treviso, core
   removed, rinsed and torn into pieces

2 tablespoons red wine vinegar

pinch of Aleppo pepper or sumac (optional)

freshly ground black pepper

"I love this dish because it's all-in-one. As simple as it sounds, coordinating eggs with sides – even for a short-order cook like me – can be a challenge!"

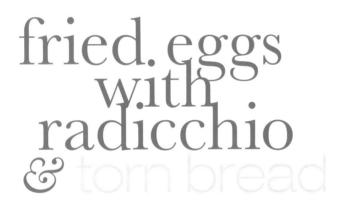

fried eggs with radicchio & torn bread

Tear the bread into small pieces. Depending on the size of your pan, you might need to cook these in two batches. Heat a frying pan over a medium-high heat until hot, then add the olive oil, bread, salt and chilli flakes. Stir until the bread is lightly toasted.

Reduce the heat to medium and break the eggs into the pan. Cook them to your liking – I prefer mine with a runny yolk.

Meanwhile, place most of the torn radicchio on a serving dish. Slide the bread and eggs from the pan onto the leaves and scatter over the rest of the radicchio. Return the pan to the heat, add the wine vinegar and swirl for a few seconds to heat. Pour over the eggs and serve, sprinkled with Aleppo and/or black pepper.

serves 4–6

1 teaspoon extra virgin olive oil

1 large onion, halved and thinly sliced

3 bacon rashers, derinded and sliced into batons

3 tablespoons dried breadcrumbs

4 medium eggs

250ml milk

170g goat's cheese or ricotta, crumbled

sea salt

freshly ground black pepper

to serve

lightly dressed baby salad leaves

"Tarts are great breakfast food, but who wants to roll out pastry in the morning? Here the breadcrumbs miraculously form a base, eliminating the need. For a richer version, use half milk and half crème fraîche or single cream."

alsatian bacon & egg tart

Preheat the oven to 200°C/Gas 6. Place a 25–26cm ovenproof frying pan over a medium heat. Add the olive oil, onion and bacon and cook until the onion is translucent, 5–10 minutes. Remove from the heat, tip the bacon and onion mixture onto a plate and set aside. Sprinkle the breadcrumbs over the base of the frying pan and scatter the bacon and onion mixture on top.

Beat the eggs and milk together in a bowl until combined. Stir through the goat's cheese, being careful not to break it up too much. Season with salt and pepper.

Pour the egg mixture over the onion and bacon in the pan. Bake for 25 minutes, or until the eggs are set and the top is lightly golden. Grind over a little more pepper and serve hot, warm or cold, as you prefer, with salad leaves.

midday fuel

The day's in full swing – there barely seems to be enough time to get everything done, let alone to feed yourself and loved ones. Lunches for me are often pulled together from freshened-up leftovers, batches of soup that last several days, or sandwiches thrown together from whatever happens to be in the fridge. When I've got the time, it will be lazy barbecues and lush salads. In the madness of the weekdays, I long for leisurely lunches, but even if it's just 15 minutes, decent food makes that short break truly restorative. I almost always take the time to sit down to have lunch. I equate eating at the desk with TV dinners. They are sometimes a fact of life, but as much as I can, I like to grab, steal and borrow that time, ideally with a loved one. It's these special moments that make life fun... those little bonuses that add a little lift to the day.

serves 4

60ml extra virgin olive oil

3 garlic cloves, crushed

6 large onions, thinly sliced

sea salt

2 teaspoons chopped oregano

2–3 tablespoons balsamic vinegar

1 litre good chicken stock

to serve

4 slices ciabatta

150g fontina cheese, thinly sliced

freshly ground black pepper

flat-leaf parsley, chopped (optional)

italian onion soup

Heat the olive oil in a large heavy-based pan over a high heat. Add the garlic and cook for 30 seconds or until fragrant. Add the onions with a little salt and cook for 7 minutes, stirring constantly. Reduce the heat to medium and continue to cook for 25 minutes or until the onions are golden brown, stirring occasionally.

Add the oregano and balsamic vinegar and cook until the vinegar has evaporated. Pour in the chicken stock and simmer for 10 minutes. (If you would like to freeze the soup, cool at this stage, then freeze in suitable containers.)

Ladle the soup into individual ovenproof soup bowls (suitable for placing under the grill) and set on a baking tray. Float a slice of ciabatta on each portion, top it with fontina and place the tray under the grill until the cheese melts. Serve immediately, sprinkled with a little pepper, and chopped parsley if you like.

"This is a re-working of the French bistro classic, but with an Italian bent. The balsamic vinegar offsets the velvety richness of the soup perfectly with its tang."

serves 4

2 tablespoons extra virgin olive oil

1 medium onion, chopped

2 celery sticks, chopped

1 large carrot, chopped

1 leek, sliced

1 thyme sprig

500ml vegetable stock

350g split peas, soaked
  in cold water for 1 hour

2 tomatoes, chopped

sea salt

freshly ground black pepper

to serve

good quality basil pesto

torn bread, fried in olive oil and
  seasoned with salt

"I'm rarely organised enough to buy a hock for pea and ham soup, but using pesto at the end does the same job as the salty ham, lifting the comforting blandness of the split peas."

split pea
soup

Heat the olive oil in a large heavy-based pan. Add the onion and cook over a medium heat for 5 minutes. Add the celery, carrot and leek, with the thyme, and cook until softened.

Pour in 1.5 litres water and the vegetable stock. Drain the soaked peas and add them to the pan with the tomatoes. Bring to a simmer and cook for 1½ hours or until the peas are soft. (If you would like to freeze the soup, cool at this stage, then freeze in suitable containers.)

Season the soup with salt and pepper to taste. Ladle into warm bowls and finish with a dollop of pesto. Serve with the fried torn bread.

serves 4

25g butter

2 medium onions, finely chopped

2 celery sticks, chopped

2 garlic cloves, finely chopped

750ml jar passata

pinch of caster sugar

500ml chicken or vegetable stock

sea salt

freshly ground black pepper

125ml single cream

"This childhood favourite is almost as easy as opening a can. Serve with farmhouse cheddar toasties and baby balsamic-pickled onions."

cream of tomato soup

Melt the butter in a large heavy-based pan over a medium heat. Add the onions and celery and cook for 15 minutes until soft, adding the garlic for the last few minutes. Add the passata, sugar, stock and seasoning. Bring to a simmer and cook for 25 minutes.

Remove from the heat and let cool slightly, then blend the soup in small batches until smooth. (If you would like to freeze the soup, cool at this stage, then freeze in suitable containers.)

Return the soup to a clean saucepan, add the cream and heat through gently without letting it come to the boil. Check the seasoning and serve.

serves 4

1 large fennel bulb, or 3 baby fennel bulbs

2 spring onions, finely sliced on the diagonal

handful flat-leaf parsley leaves

1 tablespoon good quality mayonnaise

1 tablespoon lemon juice

sea salt

freshly ground black pepper

2 tablespoons capers, rinsed and drained

1–2 teaspoons extra virgin olive oil

2 ripe avocados

12 large cooked prawns, peeled and deveined

4 slices good quality sourdough bread, toasted

lemon wedges, to serve

avocado, prawn & fennel open sandwich

Slice the fennel very finely and place in a bowl with the spring onions, parsley, mayonnaise and lemon juice. Toss together and season with salt and pepper to taste. Set aside.

Fry the capers in a little olive oil until crisp; set aside. Halve, peel and pit the avocados, then cut each half in two.

Arrange the fennel 'slaw', avocado and prawns on the toasted bread. Sprinkle with the fried capers and a little salt and pepper. Serve with lemon wedges.

"A summer favourite at my cafés. As an alternative to prawns, try smoked salmon or gravlax."

200g tinned chopped tomatoes

½ teaspoon sugar

sea salt

freshly ground black pepper

1 ciabatta, cut into 4 equal lengths and split
   horizontally

4 cooked sausages (I like Italian), sliced on the
   diagonal

1 buffalo mozzarella, 125–150g, sliced

1 tablespoon extra virgin olive oil, for drizzling

handful basil leaves

(illustrated on previous page)

"This turns that unappetising plate of cold, leftover sausages into something really scrumptious. And you can use leftover pasta sauce if you have some, rather than make the tomato sauce."

sausage, tomato & mozzarella melt

Preheat the oven to 220°C/Gas 7. Put the tomatoes in a saucepan over a medium heat, add the sugar and season with salt and pepper. Cook for 10 minutes, until the sauce is reduced and thick. Remove from the heat and allow to cool slightly.

Place the ciabatta bases on a baking tray. Spread with the tomato sauce and top with the sliced sausages and mozzarella. Grind over some pepper, drizzle with olive oil and bake for 10 minutes. Lay the ciabatta tops on the baking tray and return to the oven for a few minutes, until these slices are toasted and the cheese topping on the others is bubbling.

To serve, lay some basil leaves on the bubbling mozzarella and top with the toasted ciabatta tops.

serves 4

80ml Chinese rice wine or dry sherry

60ml oyster sauce

80ml light soy sauce

2 tablespoons caster sugar

1½ tablespoons sesame oil

4 x 150g sirloin steaks

400g asparagus, woody ends trimmed

150g bean sprouts, trimmed

1 green pepper, cored, deseeded
   and thinly sliced

1–2 small red chillies, deseeded and
   finely chopped

"If you are short of time, just marinate the beef at room temperature for half an hour."

spicy sesame beef salad

Put the Chinese rice wine, oyster sauce, 3 tablespoons soy sauce, the sugar and 1 tablespoon sesame oil in a large bowl and stir until the sugar is dissolved. Add the steaks and turn to coat. Cover with plastic wrap and leave to marinate in the fridge for 1½ hours, then at room temperature for 30 minutes.

Preheat a frying pan or barbecue until hot. Sear the steaks for 2 minutes on each side for rare, or 3–4 minutes each side for medium. Transfer them to a warm plate and allow to rest for 5 minutes in a warm place.

Blanch the asparagus in a pan of boiling water for a minute or so until bright green and tender but still crisp. Rinse under cold running water, then drain well. Toss with the bean sprouts and green pepper.

Mix together the remaining soy sauce, sesame oil and the chopped chilli. Slice each steak into 1cm slices. Divide the salad between individual plates, top with the slices of steak and drizzle over the soy/chilli dressing.

serves 4

1 tablespoon extra virgin olive oil

400g mixed mushrooms (crimini, chestnut,
 oyster etc), halved

2 spring onions, finely chopped

1 tablespoon red wine vinegar

sea salt

freshly ground black pepper

4 slices good quality bread

100g mixed baby leaves

150g goat's cheese, crumbled

50g toasted hazelnuts or candied walnuts
 (see below), roughly chopped

open sandwich of mushrooms,
& hazelnuts & goat's cheese

Heat the olive oil in a large frying pan over a medium heat. Toss in the mushrooms and stir until browned. Add the spring onions and cook for 1 minute or until they are soft. Add the wine vinegar, salt and pepper and stir through.

Toast the bread slices and top with the salad leaves and mushroom mixture. Sprinkle with crumbled goat's cheese and chopped nuts to serve.

"For candied walnuts, melt a little butter in a frying pan over medium heat and add 100g walnut halves, 55g caster sugar and 1 teaspoon cayenne pepper. Stir until the sugar melts and coats the walnuts. Spread the nuts out on a sheet of foil and leave to cool."

serves 4

300g basmati rice

2 x 180g boneless chicken breasts, skinned

1 tablespoon curry powder

5 tablespoons extra virgin olive oil

200g green beans, topped, tailed and halved

4 spring onions, finely sliced

1 celery stick, cut into batons

60g sultanas

4 tablespoons lime juice

handful coriander leaves, chopped

1 green chilli, deseeded and very finely
  diced (optional)

1 teaspoon sea salt

2 tablespoons fried sliced Asian shallots
  (optional)

to serve

lime wedges

yoghurt (optional)

salad of seared chicken & rice

Cook the rice in boiling salted water until it is cooked but still retains a slight 'bite'. Rinse under cold running water, drain well, then tip into a large bowl.

Slice the chicken into strips, place in a bowl and sprinkle with the curry powder and 2 tablespoons olive oil. Toss well to combine. Heat a frying pan over a high heat. When hot, add the chicken and cook, stirring, for about 5 minutes until cooked through. Let cool slightly.

Meanwhile, blanch the beans in a pan of lightly salted boiling water for a minute or so, until still slightly crisp. Rinse under cold running water and drain well.

Add the beans to the rice with the spring onions, celery, sultanas, remaining 3 tablespoons olive oil, lime juice, coriander, chilli and salt. Stir carefully to combine, then add the chicken and toss lightly.

Spoon the salad onto a warm platter or individual serving bowls and top with the shallots, if using. Serve with lime wedges and yoghurt if you like.

"You could use leftover shredded roast chicken and leftover rice. Just whisk the curry powder with 3 tablespoons olive oil and the lime juice and use this to dress the salad."

4 tablespoons extra virgin olive oil

1 teaspoon ground cumin

1 teaspoon ground coriander

sea salt

freshly ground black pepper

800g pumpkin, cut into small wedges and
  deseeded, skin on

1 small bunch grapes, stems removed

3 tablespoons balsamic vinegar

1 teaspoon caster sugar

2 large handfuls seasonal salad leaves, such as
  baby spinach, watercress or beetroot tops

125g soft white cheese, such as goat's curd
  or fromage frais

2 tablespoons walnuts or candied walnuts (see
  page 43), roughly chopped

pumpkin salad
with grapes & soft cheese

Preheat the oven to 220°C/Gas 7. Line a large baking tray with baking paper. Put 2 tablespoons olive oil into a large bowl with the cumin, coriander, salt and pepper, and stir to combine. Add the pumpkin wedges and toss to coat, then transfer to the baking tray. Bake for 30 minutes, or until golden brown and tender.

Heat the remaining 2 tablespoons oil in a frying pan over a medium heat. Add the grapes and cook, stirring occasionally, until slightly blistered. Add the balsamic vinegar and sugar and toss until the sugar has melted. Remove from the heat.

Arrange the pumpkin, grapes, salad leaves and soft cheese on a serving platter. Spoon over the warm dressing from the pan and sprinkle with the walnuts. Serve at once.

serves 4

600g fresh tuna, finely diced

3 spring onions, finely sliced

4 good quality anchovy fillets in oil (tinned or in
 jars), finely chopped

sea salt

freshly ground black pepper

1 tablespoon extra virgin olive oil

salad

100g chopped pitted green olives

handful flat-leaf parsley leaves

1 small red onion, finely sliced

1 tablespoon lemon juice

to serve

good quality hummus (ideally homemade)

pinch of sumac or Aleppo pepper (optional)

4 pita breads, toasted

"For perfect-shaped patties, place an egg ring or plain cutter on a board and line with plastic wrap. Place a dollop of tuna mixture in the ring and fold the plastic wrap over to enclose. Chill wrapped patties until ready to cook."

tuna burger
with olive & parsley salad

Place the tuna, spring onions and anchovies in a bowl, mix gently and season with salt and pepper (allowing for the saltiness of the anchovies). Mould into 4 burger patties, cover and refrigerate for about 1 hour.

Heat a large frying pan or griddle over a high heat (or heat up a barbecue). Add the olive oil to the pan (or brush the burgers with oil). Cook the burgers for 5 minutes on one side, then turn and cook for 2 minutes on the other side, or until browned and just cooked through.

Meanwhile, for the salad, toss the olives, parsley, onion and lemon juice together in a bowl and season to taste.

Pile the olive and parsley salad onto individual plates and top with the burgers. Add a dollop of hummus, sprinkle with sumac or Aleppo pepper, if liked, and serve with toasted pita breads.

afternoon treat

Who hasn't got dreamy memories of licking spoons and waiting expectantly by the oven to have yet another taste sensation? Sadly, now that we are so busy juggling work-family life balances, treasured baking recipes, handed down through generations, are a thing of the past. Baking, rather like letter-writing, has become something special, yet it really doesn't need to be overly complicated. You can bake with few ingredients very successfully, as my chocolate coconut slice shows, and speed up traditional methods – try my melt & mix lemon slice, for example. Biscuit doughs can be made ahead, rolled into logs and kept in the fridge, then sliced and baked on demand – tasting far better than anything you might pull from a packet. A constant abundant supply of home-baked goodies isn't realistic for most of us, but it's a shame to miss out on the inherent joy of a homemade treat – an instant shortcut to a moment of domestic bliss.

makes about 30

320g rolled oats

30g sesame seeds

45g sunflower seeds

75g chopped dried apricots

75g raisins

1 teaspoon ground cinnamon

100ml mild-flavoured oil, such as sunflower

185ml honey

"With so many schools nut-free these days, this no-nut muesli bar is ideal for the kids' lunchboxes, and not bad for grown-up ones either."

muesli bars
with apricots & sesame seeds

Preheat the oven to 180°C/Gas 4. Line a shallow 23 x 33cm baking tin with baking paper.

Place the oats, sesame seeds, sunflower seeds, dried apricots, raisins and cinnamon in a large mixing bowl and toss to mix. Put the oil and honey into a small saucepan over a medium heat and stir until melted and evenly blended.

Add the hot honey mixture to the oat mixture and stir until well combined. Press the mixture into the prepared tin and bake for 40 minutes or until golden. Remove to a wire rack and leave to cool before cutting into squares.

top: date & sultana spice bars (recipe on page 54); **below left:** muesli bars; **below right:** chocolate coconut slice (recipe on page 55)

makes about 20

300g chopped pitted dried dates

65g currants

1 teaspoon natural vanilla extract

finely grated zest of 1 lemon

185g plain flour

2 teaspoons baking powder

½ teaspoon ground cardamom

sea salt

180g soft light brown sugar

175g butter, chilled and diced

100g rolled oats

(illustrated on previous page)

date &
.sultana
spice bars

Preheat the oven to 180°C/Gas 4. Lightly grease a shallow 20 x 30cm baking tin and line with baking paper.

Put the dates, currants and 500ml water into a saucepan and bring to the boil. Reduce the heat and simmer for 15 minutes, stirring occasionally, until the mixture is thick and jammy. Stir through the vanilla extract and lemon zest. Turn off the heat and allow to cool.

Meanwhile, sift the flour, baking powder, cardamom and a pinch of salt together into a bowl, stir in the sugar and rub in the butter to form a crumbly dough; or pulse the mixture in a food processor until a dough forms. Mix through the oats.

Press half the dough into the prepared tin. Spread the date mixture evenly over the surface and crumble over the remaining dough. Bake for 40 minutes until lightly golden. Leave to cool completely in the tin. Cut into rectangles to serve.

makes about 20

250g unsweetened desiccated
  coconut
220g caster sugar
100g butter, melted and cooled
2 medium eggs, lightly beaten
150g good quality dark chocolate, chopped

(illustrated on page 53)

easiest
chocolate
coconut slice

Preheat the oven to 180°C/Gas 4. Line a shallow 30 x 20cm
baking tin with baking paper.

In a large bowl, mix the coconut and sugar together, then add
the butter and eggs and stir to combine. Stir the chopped
chocolate through the mixture and press into the prepared tin.
Bake for 20 minutes or until firm.

Leave in the tin for about 5 minutes, then cut into rectangles
and transfer to a wire rack to cool completely.

210ml soured cream

½ teaspoon bicarbonate of soda

180g butter, at room temperature

330g caster sugar

2 teaspoons finely grated lemon zest

1 teaspoon natural vanilla extract

3 medium eggs

250g blueberries (fresh or frozen)

375g plain flour

1½ teaspoons baking powder

cream cheese frosting (optional)

250g cream cheese, at room temperature

100g butter, at room temperature

1 teaspoon finely grated lemon zest

1 teaspoon natural vanilla extract

250g icing sugar, sifted

(illustrated on previous page)

"This could also be topped with a lemon drizzle icing – just mix icing sugar with lemon zest and lemon juice, then drizzle over the cake."

blueberry tea cake

Preheat the oven to 180°C/Gas 4. Grease a 23 x 33cm baking tin and line with baking paper. Mix the soured cream with the bicarbonate of soda and set aside for 5 minutes.

Beat the butter and sugar together in a bowl until light and creamy. Add the lemon zest and vanilla, and beat to combine. Beat in the eggs, one at a time, then add the soured cream mixture and mix until evenly combined.

Put the blueberries into another bowl and toss with a little of the flour. Sift the rest of the flour and baking powder over the cake mixture and carefully fold in, until just combined. Gently fold through the blueberries.

Spoon the mixture into the prepared tin and bake for 45–50 minutes, until a skewer inserted into the centre comes out clean. Leave to cool slightly in the tin for 10 minutes, then turn out and cool on a wire rack.

To make the frosting, if required, beat the cream cheese, butter, lemon zest and vanilla together in a bowl until light and fluffy, then mix in the icing sugar until smooth.

Top the cooled cake with the frosting, or serve it plain if you prefer.

makes about 20 slices

base

185g plain flour

40g cornflour

1 teaspoon baking powder

60g caster sugar

175g butter, melted

filling

600ml single cream

300g caster sugar

4 medium eggs

100g plain flour

finely grated zest of 4 large lemons

320ml lemon juice (4–6 large lemons)

melt & mix
lemon slice

Line a 23 x 33cm baking tin with baking paper. For the base, sift the flour, cornflour and baking powder into a bowl and stir in the sugar. Make a well in the centre, add the melted butter and mix well until evenly combined. Press the dough into the prepared tin and chill for 20 minutes if you have time, to help prevent shrinkage.

Preheat the oven to 180°C/Gas 4. Bake the base for 20 minutes, or until lightly golden.

Meanwhile, for the filling, whisk the cream, sugar and eggs together in a bowl. Sift the flour into another large bowl, then whisk in the cream mixture until smooth. Add the lemon zest and juice and whisk to combine.

As soon as the base is cooked, pour the filling mixture on top and return to the oven for 20 minutes or until set. Leave to cool in the tin. Cut into rectangles to serve.

makes 12

base
100g wholemeal or shortbread biscuits
55g ground almonds
50g unsalted butter, melted

filling
400g cream cheese
105ml soured cream
110g caster sugar
1 medium egg
1 medium egg yolk
½ teaspoon natural vanilla extract
1 tablespoon finely grated lime zest
50g raspberries (fresh or frozen)

to finish
extra fresh raspberries
icing sugar, to dust

individual cheesecakes

Preheat the oven to 160°C/Gas 3. Line a 12-hole, 125ml capacity muffin tin with muffin paper cases. Crush the biscuits to fine crumbs, using a food processor or rolling pin.

Put the biscuit crumbs, ground almonds and melted butter into a bowl and stir to combine. Press 1 tablespoon of the mixture into the base of each muffin case. Refrigerate while you make the filling.

To make the filling, beat the cream cheese, soured cream and caster sugar together until light and fluffy. Add the egg first, then the egg yolk, vanilla and lime zest, beating well after each addition. Spoon the mixture over the bases, then sprinkle the raspberries evenly on top.

Bake for 20 minutes or until the cheesecakes are puffed and starting to colour. Allow to cool, then refrigerate until ready to eat. .

Remove the cheesecakes from the muffin paper cases. Top each one with a fresh raspberry or two and dust with icing sugar to serve.

"Being individual, these cheesecakes don't need the overnight setting time a large one usually requires."

makes 30

140g unsalted butter, softened

40g soft light brown sugar

115g caster sugar

1 medium egg yolk

30ml treacle

150g plain flour

½ teaspoon bicarbonate of soda

1½ teaspoons ground ginger

1 teaspoon ground cinnamon

½ teaspoon ground cloves

½ teaspoon ground allspice

¼ teaspoon sea salt

demerara sugar, to coat

"These are currently my favourite biscuit. Try them with vanilla or caramel ice cream as a dessert."

crisp spice biscuits

Beat the butter and sugars together in a mixing bowl until light and fluffy. Add the egg yolk and treacle and mix well. Sift the flour, bicarbonate of soda, spices and salt together. Add to the creamed mixture and mix well until evenly combined.

Lay a sheet of plastic wrap on your work surface and form the dough into a log, 15cm long and 4cm in diameter, on top. Wrap tightly in the plastic wrap. Refrigerate for 30 minutes before slicing (or you can freeze the dough for later use).

Preheat the oven to 180°C/Gas 4. Cut the log into 5mm slices. Pour the demerara sugar into a bowl and dip the slices in – to coat one side. Place them, sugar side up, on a baking tray, spacing well apart to allow for spreading. Bake for 8–10 minutes or until dark golden.

Leave the biscuits on the baking tray for 5 minutes, then transfer to a wire rack to cool.

makes about 40

160g caster sugar

2 medium eggs

150g plain flour

60g good quality cocoa powder

80g pistachio nuts

chocolate & pistachio biscotti

Preheat the oven to 180°C/Gas 4. Line a large baking tray with baking paper.

Beat the sugar and eggs together in a bowl, using electric beaters, for 3 minutes until the mixture is thick, pale and increased in volume. Sift in the flour and cocoa powder and stir with a wooden spoon until almost combined. Add the pistachios and mix until well combined, using a clean hand.

Divide the mixture in half and shape into two logs, each about 15cm long. Place these on the prepared tray and flatten slightly until 2cm thick. Bake for 20 minutes or until firm. Remove from the oven and leave to cool completely.

Lower the oven setting to 120°C/Gas ½. Cut the logs into slices, approximately 7mm thick. Spread the slices out in a single layer on baking trays and bake for 20 minutes, turning them once halfway through cooking.

Allow the biscotti to cool completely on wire racks. Store in an airtight container for up to a month.

makes about 25

140g unsalted butter

140g pitted dried dates, finely chopped

60g good quality cocoa powder

90g plain flour

1 teaspoon baking powder

95g soft light brown sugar

3 medium eggs

1 teaspoon natural vanilla extract

healthier
chocolate
& date.
brownie

Preheat the oven to 160°C/Gas 3. Lightly grease a 20cm square baking tin and line the base with baking paper. Melt the butter in a small saucepan, add the chopped dates, take off the heat and leave to stand for 10 minutes.

Sift the cocoa powder, flour and baking powder together into a large mixing bowl. Add the brown sugar and stir to combine.

In another bowl, whisk the eggs and vanilla together, then stir in the dates and butter. Add to the dry ingredients and stir until just combined. Pour the mixture into the prepared tin and bake for 20 minutes or until set.

Turn out and cool on a wire rack, then cut into squares.

"These are a lot less calorific than your usual brownie, with most of the moisture and sweetness coming from the dates. Ideal for a more everyday treat."

makes about 12 slices

75g raisins

3 tablespoons warm tea or water

3 crisp dessert apples

250g plain flour

2 teaspoons baking powder

1 teaspoon ground allspice

1 teaspoon ground cinnamon

1 teaspoon freshly grated nutmeg

¼ teaspoon ground cloves

½ teaspoon salt

180g soft light brown sugar

60g caster sugar

250g unsalted butter, softened

3 medium eggs

1 teaspoon natural vanilla extract

85g coarsely chopped walnuts

2 teaspoons freshly grated root ginger

to serve

icing sugar, sifted, to dust

creamy yoghurt

"A bundt tin is basically a patterned ring tin, which gives the cake a very pretty decorative shape. I adore mine, but if you don't have one, try using a savarin mould or an angel cake tin."

apple fruit cake

Preheat the oven to 180°C/Gas 4. Soak the raisins in the warm tea or water in a small bowl for about 10 minutes until plump. Drain and set aside.

Lightly butter a 25cm bundt tin (or savarin mould or angel cake tin), then dust with flour, knocking out excess. Peel, core and dice the apples.

Sift the flour, baking powder, spices and salt together into a large bowl or the bowl of an electric mixer. Add the sugars, butter, eggs and vanilla. Using an electric mixer, or by hand, beat until the mixture is pale and smooth. Stir through the apples, walnuts, ginger and raisins. Spoon into the prepared tin and smooth the top.

Bake for about 1 hour until the cake is just beginning to shrink from the sides of the tin and a skewer inserted into the centre comes out clean. If the top is browning too quickly during cooking, cover loosely with foil.

Leave the cake to cool in the tin on a wire rack for 10 minutes, then invert and unmould onto the rack and cool completely.

Dust the apple cake with sifted icing sugar just before serving. Slice and serve with a dollop of creamy yoghurt.

family fare

The benefits of **eating together** as a family as often as possible are boundless. Serving **varied foods** and eating with your children from a very early age naturally encourages them to **try new flavours** and broaden their diet. This approach has really paid off with my three children, who will basically **eat anything**, or at least try everything. I also believe it's the best way to **tempt fussy eaters** to become more adventurous. And it is not just about teaching your children how to **eat well**, it is also about teaching them simple, almost **forgotten manners**, like how to use cutlery, not to chew with your mouth open, and waiting until the last person has finished eating before leaving the table. However busy and disparate our individual lives are, this is the **time to talk** and share each other's day. Enjoying meals together is the backbone of my **family life** and I cherish it.

serves 4–6

500g dried short pasta, such as
   macaroni or penne
3 tablespoons butter
3 tablespoons plain flour
875ml milk
250g gruyère or cheddar (or other
   cheese), grated
sea salt
freshly ground black pepper
140g fresh breadcrumbs
2 tablespoons extra virgin olive oil
3 tablespoons freshly grated parmesan
grated zest of ½ small lemon
handful parsley leaves, chopped

cheesy pasta
gratin

Preheat the oven to 200°C/Gas 6. Cook the pasta in a large pan of boiling salted water until al dente.

Meanwhile, melt the butter in a medium saucepan. Add the flour, stir until smooth and cook, stirring, for 1–2 minutes. Remove the pan from the heat and gradually add the milk, using a whisk to mix it through. Return to the heat and cook, stirring, until thickened. Add the cheese, stirring to melt. Season with salt and pepper to taste.

Put the breadcrumbs, olive oil, parmesan and lemon zest into a bowl and mix to combine.

Drain the pasta as soon as it is cooked and toss with the cheese sauce in an ovenproof dish. Scatter over the breadcrumb mixture and bake for 15 minutes until golden. Sprinkle with the chopped parsley to serve.

"If you are a cheese lover like me, you will probably have bits and pieces of cheeses in the fridge that are past their prime but perfect for cooking. This is a great way to use them up and introduce young palates to more adventurous flavours."

"If you can sneak it in, a handful of wilted spinach (squeezed dry, finely chopped and mixed through the beans) will turn this into an all-in-one meal."

serves 4

2 x 400g tins black beans, drained and rinsed

125g emmental, provolone or other mild
  semi-hard cheese, diced or grated

8 spring onions, finely sliced

small handful coriander leaves, chopped

sea salt

freshly ground black pepper

8 flour tortillas

2 tablespoons extra virgin olive oil

tomato salsa

500g tomatoes (ideally green)

1 small white onion, diced

3 tablespoons coriander leaves

1 green chilli, finely chopped (optional)

2 tablespoons lime juice

½ teaspoon caster sugar

½ teaspoon sea salt

quesadillas
with black beans & green tomato salsa

Put the black beans, cheese, spring onions and coriander leaves in a bowl and stir gently to combine. Season with salt and pepper to taste. Divide the mixture between the 8 tortillas, spooning it onto one side, then fold each tortilla in half.

To make the salsa, add the tomatoes to a pan of boiling water and simmer for 10–15 minutes until softened and starting to change colour. Drain the tomatoes and put them into a blender with all the rest of the ingredients. Pulse to the desired texture; I like mine quite chunky.

Preheat the oven to low. Heat a ridged griddle or frying pan over a medium heat until hot. Drizzle in 1 teaspoon olive oil, then add 2 folded quesadillas and cook for 2–3 minutes on each side until browned. Keep warm on a baking tray in the oven, while you cook the rest of your quesadillas. Serve with the tomato salsa.

serves 4

25g dried porcini mushrooms

1 litre chicken stock

1 tablespoon extra virgin olive oil

30g butter

1 small onion, finely chopped

1 garlic clove, crushed

100g pancetta, derinded and diced

250g arborio rice

80ml white wine

20g freshly grated parmesan, plus extra
  to serve

2 handfuls rocket, trimmed, roughly chopped

sea salt

freshly ground black pepper

(illustrated on previous page)

"You can try baking this risotto. While not quite as creamy, it will reward you with extra time to fit in other after-school activities. Add the stock all at once, with the parmesan, cover and bake at 200°C/Gas 6 for 30 minutes."

porcini & pancetta risotto

Soak the dried porcini in 80ml just-boiled water for 10 minutes. Drain, reserving the soaking liquid, and chop the mushrooms finely; set aside. Pour the chicken stock into a large saucepan, add the porcini liquid and bring to the boil, then reduce the heat to low and keep at a low simmer.

Heat the olive oil and half the butter in a large heavy-based pan over a medium heat. Add the onion and cook, stirring occasionally, for 5 minutes or until soft. Add the garlic and pancetta and cook, stirring from time to time, for a further 5 minutes. Add the rice and porcini and stir to coat the grains of rice in the oil. Pour in the wine and let bubble until almost completely evaporated.

Add the stock, a cupful at a time, stirring constantly and making sure that each addition of stock is absorbed before you add more. Continue adding stock for about 20 minutes or until the rice is al dente and creamy.

Remove from the heat, stir in the parmesan, remaining butter, rocket and salt and pepper to taste. Put the lid on the pan and leave to sit for 3 minutes to allow the flavours to develop. Serve with freshly ground black pepper and extra parmesan, with a big green salad on the side.

serves 4

20g dried porcini mushrooms

400g dried pappardelle (or tagliatelle)

2 tablespoons extra virgin olive oil

200g crimini or chestnut mushrooms, sliced

1 garlic clove, crushed

60ml white wine

2 large tomatoes, deseeded and finely diced

sea salt

freshly ground black pepper

2 tablespoons chopped flat-leaf parsley leaves

to serve

freshly grated parmesan

pappardelle with mushrooms, tomato & parsley

Soak the dried porcini in 125ml just-boiled water for 10 minutes. Drain, reserving 80ml of the liquid, and chop the mushrooms finely. Cook the pappardelle in a large pan of boiling salted water until al dente.

Meanwhile, heat the olive oil in a large frying pan over a medium-high heat. Add the fresh and soaked dried mushrooms and cook, stirring, for 5 minutes or until golden. Add the garlic and cook, stirring, for 1 minute.

Add the wine and bubble until reduced by half, then add the tomatoes and reserved porcini liquid and simmer for a further 2–3 minutes. Season with salt and pepper to taste and stir in the parsley.

As soon as the pasta is cooked, drain it well and toss with the sauce. Serve immediately, with freshly grated parmesan.

serves 4

4 x 180g pieces firm white fish fillet, such as
   snapper, line-caught bass or organically
   farmed cod, skinned
2 tablespoons white miso paste
2 teaspoons sugar
2 teaspoons lemon juice
2 teaspoons extra virgin olive oil

to serve
finely shredded spring onions
sesame seeds
steamed rice
steamed green vegetables, such as baby
   pak choi and asparagus

"This Japanese way of cooking fish is very simple. Cooked until well done on the surface, it has varying textures from the crisp outside to the soft inside."

miso fish
with spring onions & sesame seeds

Place the fish on a lightly oiled baking tray. Preheat the grill to high. Stir the miso paste, sugar, lemon juice and olive oil together in a bowl to combine. Brush the fish with the miso mixture and place the tray under the grill for 5–7 minutes until the fish is just cooked through.

Serve at once, sprinkled with shredded spring onions and sesame seeds. Accompany with steamed rice and green vegetables.

serves 4

1kg chicken wings

2 tablespoons fish sauce

2 garlic cloves, crushed

1 tablespoon soft brown sugar

1 teaspoon ground turmeric

satay sauce

250ml coconut cream

1 tablespoon red curry paste

100g coarsely ground dry roasted peanuts (or
  crunchy peanut butter)

1 tablespoon palm sugar (or brown sugar)

2 teaspoons soy sauce

1 tablespoon tamarind paste (or lime juice)

to serve

lime wedges

chicory or thin cabbage wedges

cucumber

blanched green beans

steamed rice

(illustrated on previous pages)

"Leftover satay sauce makes the ultimate barbecue relish."

chicken wings
with satay sauce

Cut the chicken wings into 3 pieces through the joints; reserve the wing tips for stock. In a large bowl, toss the chicken with the fish sauce, garlic, sugar and turmeric. Cover and leave to marinate in a cool place for at least 1 hour.

Preheat the oven to 220°C/Gas 7. Place the chicken on a large, shallow baking tray in a single layer and bake for 35–45 minutes or until crisp and golden.

Meanwhile, for the satay sauce, heat half the coconut cream in a small saucepan over a medium heat until just simmering. Add the curry paste and mix through until smooth and fragrant. Add the remaining ingredients with the rest of the coconut cream and continue to stir over the heat for 5 minutes until thickened.

Serve the chicken wings with lime wedges and the satay sauce. Accompany with chicory or thin cabbage wedges, cucumber, blanched green beans and steamed rice.

serves 4

125ml light soy sauce

2 teaspoons sesame oil

2 x 200g sirloin steaks, 2.5 cm thick

2 tablespoons mild-flavoured oil, such as
  sunflower

4 tablespoons Chinese black vinegar (or
  balsamic vinegar)

pinch of caster sugar

3 teaspoons chilli sambal paste (optional)

1 white onion, cut into thin wedges

1 garlic clove, crushed

200g broccoli, sprouting broccoli or broccolini,
  cut into long florets

4 celery sticks, cut into 5cm batons

to serve

2 spring onions, chopped

"If younger family members are not up to chilli yet, you could substitute a teaspoon of tomato paste for the chilli sambal paste."

sesame beef
on stir-fried celery & broccoli

Preheat the oven to 200°C/Gas 6. Mix 4 tablespoons of the soy sauce with the sesame oil in a large bowl. Add the steaks, turn to coat and allow to marinate for 10–15 minutes.

Heat a large wok or frying pan over a high heat and add 1 tablespoon oil. When hot, add the steaks and sear for 2 minutes on each side for rare steak; allow an extra minute on each side for medium; or an extra 2–3 minutes each side for well done. Transfer the steaks to a warm plate, cover loosely with foil and leave to rest in a warm place for 5 minutes.

Meanwhile, combine the remaining soy sauce, black vinegar, sugar and sambal paste, if using, in a bowl and stir to dissolve the sugar; set aside.

Return the wok to a high heat and add the remaining oil and onion. Stir-fry for 1 minute, then add the garlic and stir-fry for another 30 seconds. Add the broccoli and celery, stir-fry for 1–2 minutes, then add the soy mix and stir-fry for another minute.

To serve, slice the steaks on the diagonal. Divide the stir-fry between serving plates, top with the steak slices and scatter with chopped spring onions.

serves 4

400g thin Chinese egg noodles

100g snake beans or green beans

2 tablespoons rice vinegar, or lemon juice

60ml soy sauce

2 teaspoons sesame oil

1 teaspoon finely grated fresh root ginger

2 teaspoons sambal oelek (optional)

2 tablespoons mild-flavoured oil, such as
   sunflower

4 x 150g fish fillets, such as snapper,
   organically farmed cod or line-caught bass,
   with or without skin

sea salt

freshly ground black pepper

1 Lebanese cucumber, cut into batons

1 green pepper, cored, deseeded and
   cut into strips

handful coriander leaves

to serve
lemon wedges

"I can have this healthy, balanced, tasty meal on the table and ready to eat in just 15 minutes."

pan-seared fish
with egg noodle salad

Cook the egg noodles in boiling salted water according to the packet instructions. Drain, rinse under cold water and set aside. Cut the beans into 2cm lengths and blanch in a saucepan of lightly salted boiling water for a minute or so until still slightly crisp. Rinse under cold running water, then drain well.

In a small bowl, combine the rice vinegar, soy sauce, sesame oil, ginger and sambal oelek, if using. Add to the noodles and toss to combine.

Heat the oil in a frying pan over a high heat. Season the fish with salt and pepper. Fry the fillets (skin side down first, if appropriate) for 2–3 minutes on each side or until cooked through – this will depend on the thickness of the fillets.

Combine the noodles with the beans, cucumber, green pepper and coriander. Serve the fish with the noodle salad and lemon wedges.

serves 4

500g chicken thigh fillets, trimmed of
   excess fat

60ml soy sauce

2 tablespoons sake

1 garlic clove, crushed

2 teaspoons sugar

75g cornflour

35g plain flour

mild-flavoured oil, such as sunflower,
   for shallow-frying

to serve

salad greens

steamed sushi or short grain rice

soy sauce and hot chilli sauce, or soy sauce
   and rice vinegar, mixed together in equal
      quantities, for dipping

japanese fried chicken

Cut the chicken into bite-sized pieces. Place in a bowl with the soy sauce, sake, garlic and sugar, and toss gently to combine. Cover and leave to marinate in the fridge for at least 30 minutes.

Mix the cornflour and plain flour together in a large bowl. A piece at a time, shake off the excess sauce from the chicken and dip in the flour mixture to coat. Heat a 3–4cm depth of oil in a wok over a high heat until almost smoking. Fry the chicken, in batches, for 4 minutes or until golden. Drain on kitchen paper.

Serve immediately, with the salad greens, steamed rice and dipping sauce of your choice.

makes 2 pizzas; each serves 3

3 teaspoons dried yeast

2 tablespoons extra virgin olive oil, plus
  extra to brush and drizzle

500g strong plain white (bread) flour

2 teaspoons salt

polenta, to sprinkle

to assemble

simple tomato sauce, roasted tomato sauce
  or sun-dried tomato purée (see right)

mozzarella (preferably buffalo)

suggested toppings

basil leaves

flaked tinned tuna and Niçoise olives

prosciutto and rocket leaves

(illustrated on previous pages)

pizza

Pour 300ml tepid water into a bowl, sprinkle in the dried yeast and whisk with a fork until dissolved. Add the olive oil and set aside.

Put the flour and salt into an electric mixer fitted with a dough hook. With the mixer running on a slow speed, add all but 2 tablespoons of the yeast liquid. Add the remaining liquid (plus a dash extra if needed) to incorporate the last of the flour. Knead, still on a slow speed, for 15–20 minutes until smooth and elastic. Turn onto a floured surface and knead by hand for 1 minute to form a smooth ball. (Alternatively, mix and knead the dough entirely by hand.)

Place the dough in a lightly greased, large bowl and brush the top with a little olive oil to prevent a crust forming. Cover the bowl with plastic wrap and leave the dough to rise in a warm place for 1 hour or until doubled in size.

Preheat the oven to 230°C/Gas 8. Brush two large baking trays or pizza trays with olive oil and dust with polenta. Dust the work surface and your hands with flour. Turn the dough out onto the floured surface and divide into 2 equal pieces.

Flatten one piece out with the heels of your hands to form a rectangle shape, about 1.5cm thick. Lift the dough onto the prepared tray then, working from the centre outwards, gently stretch and press the dough into the final shape. The base should be roughly 3mm thick and the edges a bit thicker, to form a rim. Repeat to make the second base.

Spread each base with tomato sauce, using the back of a spoon, then top with slices of mozzarella. Drizzle with a little olive oil and bake for 15–20 minutes or until the base has puffed around the edges and the dough underneath is golden and crisp. Add your favourite toppings and cut each pizza into slices to serve.

"Tomato sauce is such an important cookery basic. I like to make a big batch and freeze it. Both of these sauces (but not the sun-dried purée) are freezable. Stir tomato sauce through pasta and top with torn mozzarella and pitted olives. Or, for a pre-dinner nibble, spread sun-dried tomato purée on toasted sourdough and top with ricotta."

simple tomato sauce

makes about 800ml

2 x 400g tins chopped tomatoes
2 tablespoons extra virgin olive oil
1 teaspoon sea salt
1 teaspoon sugar
freshly ground black pepper
2 garlic cloves, crushed

Tip the tomatoes into a saucepan and cook over a medium heat for 15 minutes, stirring occasionally, until reduced and thickened. Add the remaining ingredients, cook for 1 minute, then remove from the heat.

roasted tomato sauce

makes about 500ml

2kg tomatoes
60ml olive oil
few thyme sprigs
sea salt
freshly ground black pepper
1 onion, finely chopped
2 garlic cloves, crushed
2 tablespoons shredded basil

Preheat the oven to 220°C/Gas 7. Halve and core the tomatoes. Place them, cut side up, in a large roasting tray and drizzle with 2 tablespoons of the olive oil, scatter with the thyme and season with salt and pepper. Roast in the oven for 30 minutes.

Meanwhile, heat the remaining olive oil in a large saucepan over a medium-low heat. Add the onion and cook, stirring, for 5–6 minutes or until soft. Add the garlic and cook, stirring, for another minute.

Tip the roasted tomatoes and their juices into the pan and cook, stirring occasionally, for 20–30 minutes or until reduced and thick. Season to taste and stir through the basil.

sun-dried tomato purée

makes about 300ml

200g sun-dried tomatoes
about 125ml extra virgin olive oil

Process the sun-dried tomatoes in a food processor until finely chopped. With the motor running, slowly pour in the olive oil through the funnel, adding enough to give a pesto-like consistency.

the dinner dash

For all of us that have to cook every night, the weekday dinners can, at times, turn into the drudgery of groundhog day. Like everyone else, I find daily dinners to be **the biggest challenge of all**. This can be the pressure pit. En route from work, you collect the children, pick up a few things from the shops, **squeeze in** an after-school activity, plus homework and food prep. Or for those of us without kids, perhaps **work late**, find time for some exercise, and **race home** to put together a healthy, nutritious meal.

To make life yet more complicated, we have so much choice as to what to buy. No wonder we all slip into patterns of cooking the same couple of things when faced with a bewildering array of choice. But it needn't happen and variety is what makes the everyday fun. It's finding that great new wine that you are bowled over by, or that revelatory new flavour combination you haven't thought about before, that brings a sense of adventure into everyday life. These are my 30-minute dinners, and they are unashamedly fast and simple. These meals are not complicated or difficult – they're easy, straightforward flavourful dishes with just a little twist, to inspire you day to day.

serves 4

1kg roasting potatoes, such as Desirée

1 red onion, peeled and cut into wedges

75g green olives

1 lemon, sliced

50g pancetta, cut into strips

2 bay leaves

1 tablespoon tomato paste

1 tablespoon balsamic vinegar

120ml chicken stock

1 x 1.7kg chicken, jointed

1 tablespoon extra virgin olive oil

sea salt

freshly ground black pepper

chopped flat-leaf parsley (optional)

"I adore this kind of all-in-one meal that is baked and served in the same dish."

baked chicken
with lemon, potato & green olives

Preheat the oven to 180°C/Gas 4. Cut the potatoes into chunks and place in a roasting tin or ovenproof dish. Scatter over the onion, olives, lemon, pancetta and bay leaves. Stir the tomato paste and balsamic vinegar into the chicken stock, then pour over the potatoes. Lay the chicken pieces on top, drizzle with the olive oil and sprinkle with salt and pepper. Roast for 50 minutes or until the chicken is golden.

Transfer the chicken pieces to a warm plate, cover with foil and set aside to rest in a warm place. Increase the oven setting to 220°C/Gas 7 and return the roasting tin or dish to the oven for 10 minutes or until the potatoes, onion and lemon slices are well coloured.

Place the chicken back on top of the potatoes, scatter over some chopped parsley, if you like, and serve.

2 tablespoons mild-flavoured oil, such as
   sunflower
20 large raw prawns, shelled and deveined,
   with tails intact
2 tablespoons red curry paste
1 large onion, cut into thin wedges
400g asparagus, trimmed and cut into 4cm
   lengths on the diagonal
1 red pepper, cored, deseeded and cut
   into thin strips
200ml coconut milk
2 tablespoons lime juice
1 tablespoon fish sauce
1 teaspoon sugar

to serve
coriander leaves
steamed rice

(illustrated on previous pages)

"Like a cross between a curry and a stir-fry, this is rich and satisfying but still crunchy and alive."

spicy prawn
stir-fry

Heat 1 tablespoon oil in a wok or large frying pan over a high heat. Add the prawns and stir-fry for 2 minutes or until they turn pink and are just cooked. Remove and set aside.

Return the wok to a high heat, add the remaining oil, followed by the curry paste, and cook, stirring, for 1 minute or until fragrant. Add the onion and asparagus and stir-fry for 2 minutes, then add the red pepper and cook for a further 1 minute.

Add the coconut milk, lime juice, fish sauce and sugar, and stir to combine. Return the prawns to the wok and cook for a further minute or until they are heated through. Scatter over some coriander leaves and serve with steamed rice.

serves 4

600g chicken thigh fillets, trimmed of
  excess fat

3 tablespoons light soy sauce

3 tablespoons kecap manis (sweet soy)

1 tablespoon lime juice

1 tablespoon mild-flavoured oil, such as
  sunflower

1 onion, cut into thin wedges

3cm piece fresh root ginger, peeled and cut
  into thin matchsticks

150g shitake mushrooms, halved if large

1 red pepper, cored, deseeded and
  thinly sliced

200g mangetout, trimmed

to serve

chopped coriander leaves

steamed rice

"If you haven't any kecap
manis, add an extra
2 tablespoons soy sauce
and 2 teaspoons sugar."

chicken &
shitake

Thinly slice the chicken and place in a non-metallic bowl. Add
1 tablespoon light soy sauce and 2 tablespoons kecap manis, and
stir to coat the chicken in the sauce. Mix together the remaining light
soy, kecap manis and lime juice; set aside.

Heat half the oil in a large wok or frying pan over a high heat. Sear
the chicken in batches for 2–3 minutes until golden brown. Remove
and set aside.

Return the wok to a high heat and add the remaining oil, onion and
ginger. Stir-fry for 2 minutes, then add the mushrooms and stir-fry for
1 minute. Add the red pepper and mangetout, and stir-fry for a
further 1 minute.

Return the chicken to the pan, add the reserved sauce and toss until
everything is well coated in the sauce. Serve immediately, garnished
with chopped coriander and accompanied by steamed rice.

serves 4

800ml chicken stock

350ml tinned coconut milk

2 kaffir lime leaves (or 2 pieces lime zest)

3cm piece fresh root ginger, peeled and
thinly sliced

1 tablespoon fish sauce

1 tablespoon lime juice

½ teaspoon caster sugar, or to taste

4 baby pak choi, halved lengthways

dumplings

350g chicken mince

60g tinned bamboo shoots, drained
and finely chopped

2 teaspoons freshly grated root ginger

1 long red chilli, deseeded and finely
chopped

2 tablespoons chopped coriander leaves

2 teaspoons fish sauce

2 tablespoons cornflour

sea salt

freshly ground white (or black) pepper

to serve

sliced red chilli

coriander leaves

shredded kaffir lime leaves

spiced chicken
dumpling soup

To make the dumplings, put the chicken mince, bamboo shoots, ginger, chilli, coriander, fish sauce, cornflour and some salt and pepper into a large bowl. Using clean hands, mix all the ingredients together until well combined. Wet your hands and roll the mixture into small balls; set aside.

For the soup, put the chicken stock, coconut milk, kaffir lime leaves and ginger slices into a large saucepan and bring to a simmer. Reduce the heat to low, add the dumplings and simmer gently for 5 minutes or until just cooked through. Add the fish sauce, lime juice and sugar to taste. Add the pak choi, bring back to a simmer and remove from the heat.

Ladle the soup into serving bowls, dividing the dumplings evenly. Serve immediately, scattered with chilli slices, coriander leaves and shredded kaffir lime leaves.

"For a different take on this elegant soup meal, add soaked, drained rice noodles."

serves 4

4 sirloin steaks, about 2.5cm thick and
   250g each
2 tablespoons extra virgin olive oil
sea salt
freshly ground black pepper

mushroom sauce

25g butter
2 tablespoons extra virgin olive oil
2 garlic cloves, crushed
300g mixed mushrooms (crimini, oyster,
   button etc), sliced
125ml red wine
250ml beef stock
4 tablespoons crème fraîche

"Steak might seem extravagant for a midweek meal, but it cooks quickly and it's a real treat. Serve with new potatoes baked in their skins with olive oil and salt, and a mesclun and blanched green bean salad dressed with a lemony vinaigrette."

weekday steak
with mushroom sauce

Remove the steaks from the fridge and allow them to come to room temperature. Meanwhile, make the mushroom sauce. Heat the butter and olive oil in a large frying pan over a medium-high heat. Add the garlic and mushrooms and cook, stirring occasionally, for 5 minutes or until the mushrooms are golden. Add the wine and allow to bubble until reduced by half. Add the beef stock and simmer for a further 2–3 minutes or until slightly thickened. Whisk in the crème fraîche. Season with salt and pepper to taste. Keep warm.

Brush the steaks with olive oil and season liberally with salt and pepper. Heat a large frying pan over a high heat for 2 minutes. Sear the steaks for 2 minutes on each side, for rare steak. (Continue cooking over a medium heat for a further 1–2 minutes on each side for medium steaks; or for a further 2–3 minutes each side if you prefer them well done.)

Transfer the steaks to a warm plate and leave to rest in a warm place for 5 minutes. Serve them sliced, with the juices poured over and accompanied by the mushroom sauce.

serves 4–6

400ml tin coconut milk

2 tablespoons red curry paste

700g peeled, deseeded pumpkin, cut into
  3cm chunks

100g fresh or frozen peas

2 tomatoes, cut into eighths

100g baby spinach leaves

1 teaspoon brown sugar

2 teaspoons fish sauce

1 tablespoon lime juice

2 tablespoons Thai basil leaves (or chopped
  coriander)

to serve

steamed rice

"While avid fish and meat eaters, we enjoy vegetarian meals a few times a week. For an extra protein hit if you like, add cubes of firm tofu with the pumpkin."

pumpkin & pea coconut curry

Heat a wok or large saucepan over a medium heat. Pour in half the coconut milk and allow to simmer for 5–10 minutes, stirring occasionally, until it is reduced and thick. Add the curry paste and cook, stirring, for 2 minutes or until fragrant.

Add the remaining coconut milk and stir to combine. Bring to the boil, then add the pumpkin. Pour in some water as necessary, so that the pumpkin is barely covered, then return to the boil. Reduce the heat to low and simmer for 15 minutes or until the pumpkin is tender.

Add the peas and tomatoes. Simmer for 10 minutes if using fresh peas, or 5 minutes if using frozen. Add the baby spinach, sugar, fish sauce and lime juice, and stir until the spinach is wilted. Garnish with Thai basil and serve with steamed rice.

serves 4

4 x 180g skinless salmon fillets

1 teaspoon sea salt

1 teaspoon freshly ground black pepper

60ml coconut milk

1 teaspoon ground turmeric

mild-flavoured oil, such as sunflower,
  for brushing

to serve

steamed rice

steamed leafy greens

grilled coconut
salmon

Season the salmon fillets with salt and pepper. In a small bowl, stir together the coconut milk and turmeric. Brush the fish with the mixture, reserving the remainder.

Preheat a barbecue or chargrill pan on high and brush lightly with oil. Add the salmon fillets and cook for 2 minutes on each side for medium, or until cooked to your liking, brushing a little more coconut milk onto the freshly grilled surfaces.

Serve at once, with steamed rice and leafy greens.

serves 4

1 tablespoon extra virgin olive oil

1 onion, finely chopped

small handful flat-leaf parsley, chopped

2 garlic cloves, very thinly sliced

2 x 400g tins chopped tomatoes

sea salt

freshly ground black pepper

4 x 180g firm white fish fillets, such as ling,
   snapper, pollack or organically farmed cod

to serve

mashed potato

butterhead lettuce salad

oven-baked fish
with tomato &
parsley

Preheat the oven to 180°C/Gas 4. Heat the olive oil in a large ovenproof flameproof dish (with a lid) over a medium heat. Add the onion and parsley, and cook, stirring occasionally, for 5 minutes or until the onion is soft. Add the garlic and cook, stirring, for a further 1 minute.

Add the chopped tomatoes, bring to the boil, then reduce the heat to low and simmer for 10 minutes. Season with salt and pepper to taste and remove from the heat.

Add the fish to the dish, pushing the pieces into the tomato mixture. Put the lid on and cook in the oven for 15 minutes. Uncover and return to the oven for a further 10 minutes. Serve with mashed potato and a lettuce salad.

"You can add any number of flavourings to this simple recipe – chilli, finely chopped anchovies, olives and capers, for example."

serves 4

400ml ready-made dashi stock

125ml soy sauce

4 tablespoons mirin

2 tablespoons sugar

1 onion, halved and thinly sliced

4 chicken thighs, boned, skinned and diced
  (or use 2–3 skinless chicken breast fillets)

4 medium eggs, lightly beaten

to serve

steamed rice (preferably sushi or short-grain)

finely sliced spring onions or shredded
  nori, to garnish

okayodon

Pour the dashi into a medium saucepan and bring almost to the boil. Add the soy sauce, mirin and sugar, and stir to combine. Add the onion and chicken and simmer gently for 5 minutes.

Increase the heat, bring to the boil and gently pour in the beaten eggs. Cover the pan, reduce the heat to low and cook for 2 minutes.

To serve, divide the rice between 4 deep serving bowls (such as lacquered noodle bowls). Spoon the chicken, broth and egg over evenly, until the rice is moistened (you may have some broth left over).

Serve sprinkled with finely sliced spring onions or shredded nori.

"This is based on a recipe from my friend Yoko. Okayodon means 'mother and child' and this combination of chicken and egg is one of my all-time favourite dishes. It is the ultimate comfort food."

serves 4

500g good quality ready-prepared potato gnocchi
100ml chicken stock
2 tablespoons butter
100g gorgonzola cheese, crumbled
75g baby spinach leaves
freshly ground black pepper

to serve

30g walnuts, lightly toasted, chopped
chopped flat-leaf parsley

"For a change from gnocchi, try using fresh pasta, such as fettuccine or tagliatelle."

gnocchi

Cook the gnocchi in a large saucepan of lightly salted water until tender.

Meanwhile, heat the chicken stock and butter in a large pan over a medium-high heat, stirring occasionally until the butter has melted. Simmer for 2–3 minutes or until reduced by about half. Add the gorgonzola and stir until the cheese has just melted.

Drain the gnocchi as soon as they are ready and toss with the gorgonzola sauce and baby spinach. Season with pepper and serve sprinkled with the chopped walnuts and parsley.

serves 4

450g flat rice noodles (fresh or dried)

2 tablespoons mild-flavoured oil, such as
  sunflower

600g chicken mince

4 garlic cloves, crushed

200g snake beans or green beans, topped
  and cut into 3cm lengths

60ml sweet chilli sauce

60ml fish sauce

60ml dark soy sauce

60ml light soy sauce

1 tablespoon sugar

handful Thai basil leaves (or sweet basil leaves)

stir-fried rice noodles
with chicken & snake beans

Prepare the flat rice noodles according to the packet instructions.

Place a wok or frying pan over a high heat and add the oil. Add the chicken mince and brown well, stirring frequently, then add the garlic and beans. Cook, stirring, for 2 minutes.

Add all of the sauces along with the sugar and stir well. Add the prepared rice noodles and toss to combine. Remove from the heat, stir through the basil and serve in warm bowls.

"This is the replacement take-away meal. I guarantee you can make this faster than you could order and pick something up."

serves 4

4 x 150g firm white fish fillets, such as snapper,
  ling or line-caught bass, skinned
2 teaspoons sambal oelek
2 garlic cloves, sliced
2 teaspoons freshly grated root ginger
2 tablespoons soy sauce
1 tablespoon fish sauce
1 tablespoon lime juice
2 teaspoons light brown sugar

to serve
coriander leaves
lime wedges

ginger soy fish parcels

Preheat the oven to 200°C/Gas 6. Place each fish fillet on a sheet of baking paper (large enough to make a parcel). Combine all the rest of the ingredients in a bowl.

Pour the soy mixture over the fish fillets. Fold the sides of the paper over the fish and fold the edges together tightly to seal and make parcels. Place on a baking tray and bake for 15 minutes or until the fish is just cooked through.

Garnish with coriander leaves and serve with lime wedges, and accompaniments of your choice.

"Foil works just as well as baking paper for the parcels."

"Leftover sweet chilli relish will keep for several weeks sealed in a jar in the fridge. It is sublime with chicken sausages and cos lettuce in crusty rolls."

serves 4

500g piece rump steak

2 tablespoons oyster sauce

2 tablespoons soy sauce

1 tablespoon mild-flavoured oil, such as
  sunflower

sweet chilli relish

110ml mild-flavoured oil, such as
  sunflower

2 red peppers, roughly diced

2 medium red onions, roughly diced

3–4 red chillies, chopped

250g cherry tomatoes

110g sugar

125ml fish sauce

to serve

steamed greens

steamed rice

(sweet chilli relish illustrated on
previous page)

grilled beef
with sweet
chilli relish

Remove the steak from the fridge and allow to come to room
temperature. Meanwhile, prepare the relish. Heat the oil in a medium
saucepan over a medium heat. Add the red peppers, onions and
chillies, and fry, stirring occasionally, for about 20 minutes until
browned, reducing the heat if the vegetables begin to catch. Add the
tomatoes and simmer for 5–7 minutes until softened. Add the sugar
and fish sauce and simmer until thickened and caramelised. Let cool
slightly, then purée in a food processor. Transfer to a bowl and set
aside. (You will have more relish than you need for this recipe.)

Combine the oyster and soy sauces and rub all over the meat. Heat
a griddle or heavy-based frying pan over a medium-high heat (or you
can use a barbecue). Brush the meat lightly with oil and place on the
griddle. Cook for about 3 minutes on the first side, then turn and
cook for 2 minutes on the other side for medium-rare.

Transfer the steak to a warm plate, cover with foil and set aside to
rest for 10 minutes. Slice the beef thinly and serve with the chilli
relish, steamed greens and rice.

serves 4

4 pork loin chops, trimmed of excess fat

extra virgin olive oil, to brush

1 teaspoon sweet paprika

sea salt

freshly ground black pepper

warm rice salad

2 tablespoons extra virgin olive oil

1 small onion, grated or finely chopped

200g basmati rice

440ml chicken stock

1 bay leaf

2 fresh corn cobs, kernels stripped

200g green beans, cut into 1cm lengths

small handful coriander sprigs

tomato salsa

3 tomatoes, deseeded and diced

½ red onion, finely diced

handful coriander leaves

2 tablespoons lime juice

pork chops
with rice salad & salsa

For the rice salad, heat the olive oil in a medium saucepan (with a tight-fitting lid) over a low heat. Add the onion and cook, stirring, for 2–3 minutes or until softened. Add the rice and stir to coat with the oil, then add the stock and bay leaf. Bring to the boil, reduce the heat to low, cover tightly and cook for 10 minutes. Add the corn kernels and beans and cook for a further 5 minutes or until the vegetables are tender and all the liquid has been absorbed.

Meanwhile, heat a large frying pan over a high heat. Brush both sides of the chops with olive oil and sprinkle with the paprika, salt and pepper. Cook for 3–5 minutes on each side, according to thickness, then remove from the heat. Cover with foil and set aside to rest in a warm place for 10 minutes. Leave the rice salad to rest for 5 minutes, then season with salt and pepper and stir through the coriander.

Meanwhile, combine all the tomato salsa ingredients together in a bowl and season with salt and pepper to taste. Serve the pork chops with the tomato salsa and warm rice salad.

serves 4

400g dried penne

3 tablespoons extra virgin olive oil

400g baby squid with tentacles, cleaned and
  cut into strips

125g chorizo sausage, diced

1 tablespoon tomato paste

3 garlic cloves, sliced

1 green chilli, sliced

250g cherry tomatoes, halved

4 spring onions, sliced

2 tablespoons sherry or red wine vinegar

sea salt

freshly ground black pepper

handful flat-leaf parsley, chopped

"The trick here is not to touch the squid while it sears and colours, and to turn it only once. If you stir it frequently, it will stew and turn rubbery."

penne with squid & chorizo

Cook the pasta in a large pan of boiling salted water until al dente.

Meanwhile, heat the olive oil in a large frying pan. Add the squid and cook, for 2 minutes, without stirring, then turn and cook for 1 minute on the other side; do not overcook. Remove from the pan and set aside.

Add the chorizo to the frying pan and cook, stirring, for about 2 minutes until golden. Add the tomato paste, garlic and chilli, and stir over the heat for another minute, then add the cherry tomatoes and spring onions. Cook, stirring, until the tomatoes are softened.

Drain the pasta as soon as it is ready, reserving about 60ml of the cooking liquid. Add the pasta to the sauce with the squid and vinegar. Stir to combine, adding the reserved cooking liquid to loosen the sauce slightly if necessary. Season with salt and pepper to taste and stir through the chopped parsley to serve.

2 x 800g (or a 1.5kg) white fish,
  such as small bass, cleaned and scaled
handful coriander leaves
10 spring onions, chopped
1 teaspoon chilli flakes
2 tablespoons extra virgin olive oil
1 teaspoon salt

lemon potatoes
1kg yellow waxy potatoes
3 tablespoons extra virgin olive oil
3 garlic cloves, crushed
sea salt
freshly ground black pepper
125ml fish or chicken stock
60ml lemon juice
100g pitted black olives,
  roughly chopped
small handful flat-leaf parsley, finely
  chopped

"Whole fish can seem daunting for novice cooks, but here it is easy to handle. With the protective herb paste coating, you can just pop the whole thing in the oven."

baked
whole fish
with lemon potatoes

Preheat the oven to 200°C/Gas 6. For the lemon potatoes, cut the potatoes into thick slices and place in a roasting tray. Add the olive oil, garlic, salt, pepper, stock and lemon juice, and toss with your hands to combine. Bake in the oven for 25 minutes, stirring every 10 minutes.

Meanwhile, make 3 slashes on each side of the fish through the thickest part and place on a baking tray. Put the remaining ingredients into a food processor and process to a coarse paste. Spread the paste over each side of the fish and into the slashes.

Lower the oven setting to 180°C/Gas 4 and put the fish into the oven (below the potatoes). Bake for 20 minutes or until it is cooked through, adding the olives and parsley to the potatoes for the last 5 minutes. Serve at once, placing the fish on top of the potatoes if you like.

serves 4

10 medium eggs

2 garlic cloves, crushed

2 teaspoons freshly grated root ginger

2 teaspoons Chinese rice wine

4 tablespoons mild-flavoured oil, such as
  sunflower

300g Chinese barbecued pork, thinly sliced
  (or use cooked shredded chicken)

2 handfuls mangetout, finely sliced on
  the diagonal

75g bean sprouts, trimmed

6 spring onions, finely sliced

to serve

oyster sauce

steamed rice

chinese style omelette
with barbecued pork

In a bowl, whisk together the eggs, garlic, ginger and rice wine. Heat 2 tablespoons of the oil in a large frying pan or wok over a high heat. Add half the egg mixture and cook, pushing the uncooked egg mixture to the sides.

When the omelette is almost set, scatter half of the pork, mangetout, bean sprouts and spring onions along the middle. Carefully fold each side of the omelette over to enclose the filling. Slide from the wok onto a serving plate. Keep warm while you cook the second omelette.

To serve, halve the omelettes and drizzle with oyster sauce. Accompany with steamed rice.

"Elizabeth David's 'An Omelette and a Glass of Wine' encapsulates a certain elegance of the most simple meal. Try this omelette with an icy cold beer."

serves 4

1 x 1.5kg chicken, jointed into 8 pieces
2 tablespoons red curry paste
190ml coconut milk
2 tablespoons fish sauce
1 tablespoon brown sugar
400g tin chopped tomatoes

to serve

basil and coriander leaves (optional)
lime wedges
Indian breads
cucumber, watercress and onion salad

roast chicken curry

Preheat the oven to 190°C/Gas 5. With a sharp knife, slash the thickest parts of the chicken legs and thighs so they will cook evenly. In a large bowl, combine the curry paste, coconut milk, fish sauce and brown sugar. Place the chicken pieces in a baking tray (in which they fit quite snugly) and pour over the curry coconut mixture. Leave to marinate for at least an hour, or overnight if time permits.

Add the tomatoes and gently mix through. Bake for 40 minutes or until the chicken is browned and the juices run clear when the thickest parts are pierced with a skewer. (Finish under the grill to brown if necessary.)

Scatter some basil and coriander leaves over the curry, if you like, and serve with lime wedges for squeezing. Accompany with warm Indian breads and salad.

"Serve this with a quick salad of watercress, cucumber and finely sliced white onion (pre-soaked in water for 5 minutes and drained)."

serves 4

500g sweet potato

1 tablespoon extra virgin olive oil, plus
   extra to brush

sea salt

freshly ground black pepper

4 pork medallions

warm cranberry dressing

60ml Marsala (or port)

250ml chicken stock

40g dried cranberries

to serve

200g green beans, topped and blanched

1 bunch watercress

40g pistachio nuts, chopped

grilled pork
with warm cranberry dressing & pistachios

Preheat the oven to 200°C/Gas 6. Cut the sweet potato into large chunks and toss in a bowl with 1 tablespoon olive oil and some salt and pepper. Place on a large baking tray and bake for 20 minutes.

Heat a heavy-based frying pan over a high heat. Brush the pork medallions with olive oil and season liberally with salt and pepper. Sear in the hot pan for 1 minute on each side, then place the pork on the baking tray with the sweet potato. Cook in the oven for a further 10 minutes. Save the juices in the frying pan.

Transfer the pork to a warm plate, cover with foil and set aside to rest in a warm place for 10 minutes. Return the sweet potato to the oven while the pork is resting. Meanwhile, for the dressing, add the Marsala to the frying pan and stir over a medium-high heat for 30 seconds to deglaze. Pour in the chicken stock and let bubble to reduce for 5 minutes, then add the cranberries and cook for 1 minute.

Place the green beans and watercress on serving plates or a platter. Slice each pork medallion into three and arrange on top. Pour the cranberry sauce over the pork and sprinkle with chopped pistachios. Serve with the roasted sweet potato.

1 bunch asparagus, woody ends trimmed
40g baby spinach leaves
50g skinned almonds, lightly toasted
2 garlic cloves
40g parmesan, freshly grated
1 teaspoon finely grated lemon zest
80ml extra virgin olive oil
sea salt
freshly ground black pepper
2 tablespoons lemon juice
400g dried fettuccine (or tagliatelle)
60ml single cream

to serve
freshly grated parmesan

"When asparagus isn't in season, substitute blanched broccoli."

fettuccine with asparagus pesto

Blanch the asparagus in a large saucepan of lightly salted boiling water until bright green and tender yet crisp. Drain and rinse under cold running water to cool completely, then drain well. Cut off the asparagus tips and reserve.

Put the blanched asparagus stalks, spinach leaves and almonds into a food processor with the garlic, parmesan and lemon zest, and pulse until finely chopped. With the motor running, slowly add the olive oil through the funnel, processing until you have a smooth consistency. Season with salt and pepper to taste and stir through the lemon juice.

Cook the fettuccine in a large saucepan of lightly salted water until al dente. Drain and return to the saucepan. Add the asparagus pesto, cream and reserved asparagus tips. Toss to combine and check the seasoning. Serve immediately, with extra parmesan.

2 tablespoons extra virgin olive oil

1 large onion, finely chopped

1 teaspoon ground coriander

1 teaspoon ground cumin

1 teaspoon ground turmeric

½ teaspoon cayenne pepper

400g tin chopped tomatoes

10–15 fresh curry leaves

sea salt

250ml chicken or fish stock

1 teaspoon caster sugar

juice of 1 lime

900g skinless salmon fillet

freshly ground black pepper

to serve

watercress or coriander leaves

finely sliced white onion

steamed rice

"When you feel like a quick, spicy hit to brighten up a chilly winter night, this salmon curry fits the bill. It's a fast, fresh, healthy way to cook a fish fillet."

indian style
salmon curry with tomato & lime

Heat the olive oil in a large heavy-based pan over a medium-low heat. Add the onion and cook, stirring occasionally, for 5 minutes or until translucent. Add the ground coriander, cumin and turmeric, and cook, stirring, for another 2 minutes or until fragrant.

Add the cayenne, tomatoes, curry leaves and 1 teaspoon salt, then pour in the stock. Cook, stirring frequently, for 10 minutes. Add the sugar and lime juice and cook for 1–2 minutes.

Meanwhile, cut the salmon into 3cm cubes. Add to the pan and simmer for 2–3 minutes, then remove from the heat. Set aside for 5 minutes to allow the salmon to finish cooking in the residual heat. Season with salt and pepper to taste.

Garnish with watercress or coriander leaves and finely sliced white onion. Serve with steamed rice.

serves 4

4 x 200g pork loin steaks
extra virgin olive oil, to brush
sea salt
freshly ground black pepper

cashew nut salsa

1 large cucumber
60ml lime juice
1 tablespoon fish sauce
1 teaspoon sugar
2 coriander roots, finely chopped
65g roasted unsalted cashews,
  chopped
small handful coriander leaves, chopped
1 red chilli, finely chopped

to serve

blanched asparagus
iceberg lettuce

pork steaks

For the salsa, halve, peel, deseed and finely dice the cucumber. Place in a bowl with all the other ingredients and toss to mix. Set aside.

Heat a griddle or heavy-based frying pan over a high heat. Brush the pork steaks with olive oil and season well with salt and pepper. Cook for 3–4 minutes on each side, depending on thickness, until cooked through.

Serve the pork steaks with the asparagus, lettuce and cashew nut salsa.

"I like to make the cashew salsa before cooking the steaks, to give the flavours time to meld and soften."

2 large aubergines

3 tablespoons extra virgin olive oil,
  plus extra to brush

1 red onion, chopped

1 teaspoon ground coriander

1 teaspoon ground cumin

1 teaspoon ground cinnamon

1 teaspoon paprika

400g tin chopped tomatoes

4 garlic cloves, crushed

1 green chilli, finely chopped

1 teaspoon sugar

1 tablespoon lime juice

sea salt

freshly ground black pepper

4 x 150g tuna steaks

to serve

coriander and mint leaves

"Serve with flatbreads – brushed with a little olive oil, sprinkled with fennel seeds, sea salt and black pepper, and baked at 220°C/Gas 7 for 10 minutes."

spiced tuna
with moroccan relish

Preheat the oven to 200°C/Gas 6. Cut the aubergines into cubes and toss with 2 tablespoons olive oil. Place in a single layer on a baking tray and roast for 30 minutes or until well coloured, turning occasionally.

Heat the remaining olive oil in a large frying pan over a medium heat. Add the onion and cook until softened. Sprinkle in the ground spices and cook, stirring, for 1 minute. Add the tomatoes, garlic and chilli, and bring to a simmer. Now add the aubergine and cook for 5 minutes or until the sauce is thickened. If it seems too thick, add a little water to thin. Add the sugar, lime juice and salt and pepper to taste.

Brush the tuna steaks with olive oil and season with salt and pepper. Preheat a griddle or heavy-based frying pan over a medium-high heat. Add the tuna steaks and cook for 3 minutes on each side, ensuring they remain pink in the centre.

To serve, divide the aubergine relish between serving plates and top with the tuna steaks. Garnish with mint and coriander leaves.

serves 4

4 x 160g boneless chicken breasts, skinned

125g plain flour

4 teaspoons sweet paprika

2 teaspoons ground cumin

1 tablespoon finely chopped thyme leaves

1 teaspoon sea salt

freshly ground black pepper

2 medium egg whites, lightly beaten

60ml extra virgin olive oil

to serve

lemon wedges

mashed potato

green salad

crispy crusted chicken breasts

Slice the chicken breasts in half horizontally. In a large bowl, mix the flour with the paprika, cumin, thyme, salt and pepper. Dip the chicken breasts into the flour mixture, then into the beaten egg whites, then into the flour mixture again to coat thoroughly. Repeat to coat the rest of the chicken.

You may need to cook the chicken in two batches. Heat the olive oil in a large frying pan over a medium heat. Add the chicken in a single layer, being careful not to crowd the pan. Cook for 3 minutes, then turn and cook for 2 minutes on the other side until the chicken breasts are golden and cooked through.

Serve the chicken breasts with lemon wedges, mashed potato and a green salad.

serves 4

800g boneless roasting beef joint, such
  as topside
extra virgin olive oil, for drizzling
sea salt
freshly ground black pepper

spelt salad
180g spelt
500ml chicken stock or water
250g cherry tomatoes, quartered
handful basil leaves, roughly torn
handful flat-leaf parsley leaves
3 spring onions, finely chopped
1 tablespoon extra virgin olive oil

tapenade
120g pitted black olives, finely chopped
4 good quality anchovy fillets in oil (tinned
  or in jars), finely chopped
1 teaspoon Dijon mustard
1 tablespoon lemon juice
2 tablespoons chopped flat-leaf parsley
1 garlic clove, crushed
60ml extra virgin olive oil

"As this tapenade is diced rather than pounded, it has a light touch, and doesn't overpower the delicate flavour of the spelt and the sweet tomatoes."

roast beef
with spelt salad & tapenade

Preheat the oven to 220°C/Gas 7. Place the beef in a large roasting tray, drizzle with olive oil and season with salt and pepper. Roast in the oven for 10 minutes or until browned. Reduce the heat to 200°C/Gas 6 and roast the beef for a further 20 minutes (it will be medium-rare). Remove from the oven, cover loosely with foil and set aside to rest for 20 minutes.

Meanwhile, for the salad, put the spelt and chicken stock into a small saucepan and bring to the boil. Cover, reduce the heat to low and simmer for 20–25 minutes until the liquid has been absorbed. Remove from the heat and leave to rest, covered, for 5 minutes.

For the tapenade, place all the ingredients in a bowl and stir to combine.

Transfer the spelt to a bowl and allow to cool for 10 minutes or so. Scatter over the tomatoes, basil, parsley and spring onions, and drizzle with a little olive oil.

Slice the beef thinly and serve with the spelt salad and tapenade.

on a shoestring

We all have a need, sometimes, to tighten our belts – whether it's to get to the next payday or to save for the mortgage, school fees or even a night out with friends. Very few of us escape financial pressure. Despite what you read in glossy magazines and supplements, good food is not about glamorous, expensive restaurants, it is about the intrinsic pleasure of food and everything about it, including the fun of cooking. Cheaper food doesn't mean bad food. Pulses are cheap, comforting and fortifying, so too are pasta, rice and flavourful vegetables. And of course, there are those less expensive robust cuts of meat. They may start off tough, but gentle low-temperature coaxing, over a considerable time, transforms them into the most succulent, tender, melt-in-the-mouth experience When times are challenging, there's no need to be meagre when it comes to feeding yourself, friends and loved ones... but don't just save these recipes for lean times – enjoy them as often as you can.

serves 4

400g dried spaghetti

125ml extra virgin olive oil

3 garlic cloves, very thinly sliced

½ teaspoon dried chilli flakes

8 good quality anchovy fillets in oil (tinned
  or in jars), chopped

300g turnip tops (*cime di rape*), or other
  bitter greens, such as mustard greens

freshly ground black pepper

to serve

freshly grated parmesan

spaghetti
with anchovies
& turnip tops

Cook the spaghetti in a large pan of lightly salted boiling until al dente.

Meanwhile, heat the olive oil in a large frying pan over a medium heat. Add the garlic, chilli flakes and anchovies. Cook, stirring, for 2 minutes, until starting to colour. Add the turnip tops and cook, stirring occasionally, for a few minutes, until just wilted.

Drain the pasta as soon as it is ready. Add to the frying pan and toss gently. Season with pepper and serve immediately, with grated parmesan for sprinkling.

"As a cheaper alternative to parmesan, fry some thin slices of sourdough or ciabatta in olive oil until crisp. Cool, then crumble over the pasta to serve."

serves 4

2 tablespoons extra virgin olive oil

2 onions, diced

2 teaspoons freshly grated root ginger

2 garlic cloves, crushed

1 teaspoon ground cumin

1 teaspoon ground turmeric

1½ teaspoons ground cinnamon

1kg carrots, sliced

1.5 litres chicken stock

1 teaspoon brown sugar

1 tablespoon lime juice

sea salt

to serve

yoghurt

sumac, to sprinkle

(preparing the soup illustrated
on previous pages)

"For a thicker soup, add a good handful of basmati rice along with the carrots."

spiced carrot soup
with lime

Heat a large cooking pot over a medium-high heat and add the olive oil. Tip in the onions and cook gently, stirring occasionally, until translucent. Add the grated ginger, garlic and spices, and stir for a couple of minutes until fragrant. Add the carrots and chicken stock, and bring to the boil. Reduce the heat to a simmer and cook for 30 minutes or until the carrots are soft.

Remove from the heat and purée the soup using a hand-held stick blender, taking care as it will be very hot. Reheat if required, and stir though the sugar, lime juice and salt to taste.

Divide the soup between warm bowls and serve topped with a dollop of yoghurt and a sprinkling of sumac.

8 chicken drumsticks

80ml soy sauce

2 tablespoons lime juice

3 garlic cloves, crushed

2 teaspoons ground cumin

1 teaspoon paprika

1 small red chilli, deseeded and finely chopped

to serve

warm rice salad (see page 119)

chicken drumsticks
with paprika & garlic

Using a sharp knife, make a few slashes through the thicker parts of the chicken and place in a dish. Combine all the remaining ingredients in a small bowl. Using your hands, rub this marinade all over the chicken drumsticks. Leave to marinate for at least an hour, or overnight if time permits.

Preheat the oven to 190°C/Gas 5 (or preheat a barbecue). Place the chicken in a baking tray and roast, uncovered, for 40 minutes or until well coloured and cooked through. Serve with a warm rice salad.

serves 4

500g dried bucatini (or rigatoni)

225g peas (fresh or frozen)

60ml extra virgin olive oil

100g pancetta, chopped

4 medium eggs

115g ricotta

40g parmesan, freshly grated

freshly ground black pepper

sea salt

"This is a new take on spaghetti carbonara. The ricotta mixed with the eggs gives a richness that is incredibly satisfying, and the peas add a delectable sweetness."

bucatini with peas, pancetta & ricotta

Cook the pasta in a large pan of boiling salted water until al dente, according to the packet instructions. Add fresh peas 5 minutes before it will be cooked al dente; add frozen peas just 2 minutes before.

While the pasta is cooking, heat the olive oil in a large frying pan over a medium-high heat. Add the pancetta and cook until lightly crisp. Meanwhile, lightly whisk the eggs, ricotta and parmesan together in a bowl.

Drain the pasta and peas as soon as they are ready and return to the pan. Add the pancetta, then the egg and ricotta mixture and stir though. Add lots of pepper, and salt to taste. Serve immediately.

serves 4

1.2kg piece boned shoulder of lamb,
  trimmed of excess fat

80ml extra virgin olive oil

3 garlic cloves, crushed

4 rosemary sprigs

2 bay leaves

sea salt

freshly ground black pepper

1 small onion, finely diced

2 x 400g tins chopped tomatoes

2 x 400g tins cannellini beans, rinsed and
  drained

small handful chopped flat-leaf parsley, or
  other herb of your choice

slow-cooked lamb shoulder
with white beans

"Finishing the lamb off in a hot oven gives the surface a crisp and chewy contrast to the soft tender meat underneath."

Preheat the oven to 160°C/Gas 3. Place the lamb shoulder in a baking dish. Mix all but 1 tablespoon of the olive oil with the garlic, rosemary and bay leaves, and rub over the lamb. Season with salt and pepper, then pour a cup of water into the dish and cover tightly with foil. Bake in the oven for 3 hours.

Remove the foil and increase the oven setting to 230°C/Gas 8. If there is more than ½ cup of liquid in the dish, drain some off. Return the lamb to the oven for 15–20 minutes or until the surface is browned and crisp.

Meanwhile, heat the remaining 1 tablespoon olive oil in a pan over a medium heat, add the onion and fry gently until soft. Tip in the tomatoes and cannellini beans, bring to a simmer and cook gently for 30 minutes, adding a little water as necessary.

When the lamb is ready, cover with foil and rest in a warm place for 15 minutes. Add the parsley to the beans and season with salt and pepper to taste. Slice the lamb and serve with the beans.

serves 4

1 tablespoon extra virgin olive oil

sea salt

freshly ground black pepper

6 lamb chump chops, trimmed of fat

2 red onions, finely sliced

2cm piece fresh root ginger, grated

4 garlic cloves, sliced

1 red chilli, finely chopped

1 tablespoon ras al hanout

5 tomatoes, diced (or 400g tin chopped
  tomatoes)

800g sweet potatoes, peeled and cut
  into large chunks

2 tablespoons lemon juice, or to taste

1 tablespoon soy sauce

1 tablespoon honey

1 cinnamon stick

to serve

steamed couscous or rice

handful coriander leaves

"Freshen up this slow-cooked dish with a crunchy radish and minted cucumber salad."

lamb chops

with sweet potatoes & lemon

Preheat the oven to 180°C/Gas 4. Heat the olive oil in a flameproof casserole over a medium-high heat. Season the lamb chops liberally with salt and pepper, and brown on both sides. Remove the chops and set aside.

Drain off all but 1 tablespoon oil from the casserole and reduce the heat to medium. Add the onions and cook, stirring, until softened, about 5 minutes. Now add the ginger, garlic, chilli and ras al hanout, and stir for a couple of minutes until fragrant. Add the tomatoes and stir over the heat for another 5 minutes.

Add the browned lamb chops, sweet potatoes, lemon juice, soy sauce, honey and cinnamon. Pour in about 400ml water, or just enough to cover your chops. Put the lid on and cook in the oven for 2 hours.

Uncover and skim off any excess fat from the surface. If the sauce is too thin, reduce over a medium-high heat for a few minutes. Adjust the seasoning – you may need an extra squeeze of lemon juice. Serve with steamed couscous or rice, scattering over some coriander leaves.

serves 4

2kg pork shoulder on the bone

6 shallots, peeled

6 garlic cloves, peeled

5cm piece fresh root ginger, grated

3 tablespoons soy sauce

4 tablespoons kecap manis (sweet soy)

1 teaspoon ground white pepper

2 tablespoons extra virgin olive oil

4 red chillies

1 cinnamon stick

3 star anise

500ml chicken stock

pineapple salad

400g pineapple, peeled, cored and diced

2 spring onions, finely sliced

1 small red chilli, deseeded and finely
  chopped (optional)

handful coriander leaves

1 tablespoon fish sauce

1 tablespoon brown sugar

2 tablespoons lime juice

"This recipe makes enough for leftovers. Serve in baguettes – Vietnamese-style – along with grated carrot, cos lettuce and hoisin sauce."

braised pork
with pineapple salad

Preheat the oven to 180°C/Gas 4. Place the pork in a roasting tray. Put the shallots, garlic, ginger, soy, kecap manis, pepper and olive oil into a food processor and blend to form a paste. Rub all over the surface of the pork.

Add the chillies, cinnamon and star anise to the roasting tray and pour in the stock. Moisten a large sheet of baking paper with water and place over the pork. Cover the tray tightly with foil and roast for 2 hours.

Increase the oven setting to 220°C/Gas 7. Take out the pork and baste with the pan juices. Return, uncovered, to the oven for 20 minutes or until well coloured.

Meanwhile, to prepare the salad, combine the pineapple, spring onions, chilli and coriander leaves in a bowl. For the dressing, mix together the fish sauce, sugar and lime juice, then pour over the salad and toss to mix.

Rest the pork in a warm place for 10 minutes before slicing. Serve with the pineapple salad.

serves 4

2kg rack of pork back ribs
4 garlic cloves, crushed
2 tablespoons freshly grated root
  ginger
125ml soy sauce
125ml hoisin sauce
60ml honey
1 teaspoon five-spice powder
2 tablespoons mild-flavoured oil,
  such as sunflower

cabbage salad
¼ cabbage, cored
2 tablespoons white wine vinegar
few drops of sesame oil
sea salt
½ teaspoon sugar

to serve
steamed rice

(illustrated on previous pages)

sticky.
five-spice ribs

Put the pork ribs in a baking dish. Place all the rest of the ingredients in a food processor and pulse until smooth, or simply stir together in a bowl to combine. Pour all but a few tablespoons of this marinade over the ribs and rub well in. Turn the ribs meat-side down, ready for cooking.

Preheat the oven to 200°C/Gas 6. Bake the pork ribs for 40 minutes, then turn them over and brush with the reserved marinade. Increase the oven setting to 220°C/Gas 7 and cook for a further 10 minutes.

Meanwhile, for the salad, shred the cabbage and place in a bowl. Combine the wine vinegar, sesame oil, salt and sugar to make a dressing. Drizzle over the cabbage and toss with your hands to mix.

Lift the ribs onto a board and cut each rib off the rack separately. Serve with the cabbage salad and steamed rice.

"These pork ribs can also be barbecued on a hot grill."

serves 4

4 thick-cut pork neck chops, about 1.5kg in total

sea salt

freshly ground black pepper

3 tablespoons extra virgin olive oil

8 baby onions, peeled

250ml white wine

4 garlic cloves, lightly crushed with a knife

500g celeriac, peeled and cut into large chunks

750ml chicken stock

1 cinnamon stick

150g prunes, pitted

60ml single cream

1 teaspoon Dijon mustard

2 tablespoons chopped parsley

"This delicious midwinter dish calls for some barely steamed Brussels sprouts, drizzled with a little olive oil. That's all."

pork with mustard,
celeriac & prunes

Preheat the oven to 160°C/Gas 3. Season the pork chops generously with salt and pepper. Heat the olive oil in a large ovenproof pan over a high heat. Brown the pork on both sides; you will need to do this in two batches.

Return all the meat to the pan, add the onions and toss until golden. Pour in the wine, stirring to deglaze. Add the garlic and celeriac, pour over the chicken stock, then add the cinnamon and prunes. Cover with a sheet of baking paper, then a tight-fitting lid or foil. Cook in the oven for 1½ hours.

Using a slotted spoon, transfer the pork and vegetables to a warm dish and cover to keep warm. Place the pan on the hob over a medium-high heat to reduce the liquid slightly, then stir through the cream, mustard and chopped parsley. Spoon over the pork and vegetables to serve.

1kg chuck or blade steak

3 tablespoons plain flour

2 teaspoons paprika

1 teaspoon sea salt

freshly ground black pepper

400g tin chopped tomatoes

1 large onion, halved and finely sliced

300g carrots, peeled and chopped

3 large garlic cloves, sliced

3 good quality anchovy fillets in oil (tinned or in jars), finely chopped

4 sage leaves, finely chopped

170ml red wine

2 sheets ready-made butter puff pastry

1 egg yolk, lightly beaten

to serve

good quality tomato chutney

green salad

mashed potato and celeriac

"The success of this recipe lies in its simplicity; you don't have to brown the meat at all and the oven does all the work for you."

beef pot pie

Preheat the oven to 180°C/Gas 4. Cut the beef into 2cm chunks. Put the flour, paprika, salt and pepper in a bowl and stir to combine. Add the beef and toss to coat, then transfer to a casserole dish. Add the tomatoes, onion, carrots, garlic, anchovies, sage and red wine and stir to mix. Cover and cook in the oven for 2 hours, stirring occasionally, or until the sauce has thickened slightly and the beef and carrots are tender.

You will need a 2 litre pie dish or 6 x 200ml individual pie dishes or large ramekins. Using a dish upside-down as a guide, cut out round(s) of pastry for the pie lid(s), allowing an extra 1cm all round.

Spoon the beef filling into the pie dish(es) and cover with the pastry lid(s), pushing down the edges around the rim. Make a slit in the top with a sharp knife. You can refrigerate the pie(s) at this stage if preparing ahead.

When ready to cook, brush the pastry with egg yolk and bake the pie(s) in the oven until the crust is lightly golden; allow 35–40 minutes for a large pie; 20–25 minutes for individual pies.

Serve with tomato chutney and a green salad, or for a more substantial meal, with mashed potato and celeriac as well.

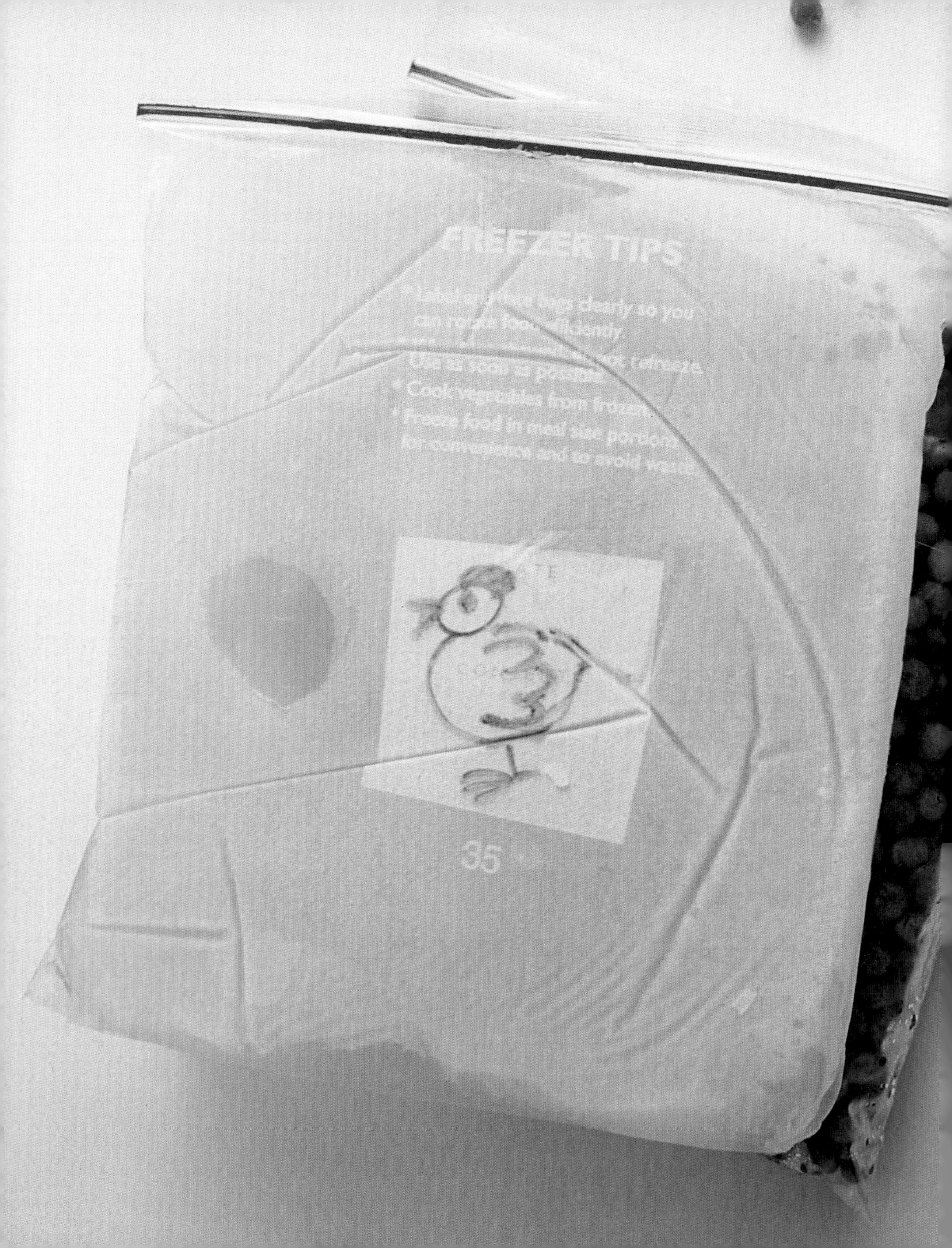

FREEZER TIPS

* Label and date bags clearly so you
  can rotate food efficiently.
* .... not refreeze.
  Use as soon as possible.
* Cook vegetables from frozen.
* Freeze food in meal size portions
  for convenience and to avoid waste.

35

freeze me

When there is no time to shop, or it is difficult to leave the house, a freezer full of food that is ready to go, to heat and serve, is a godsend in my life. Homemade curries, braises, pies and soups are great standbys that certainly don't suffer from a holiday in the freezer. And frozen homemade stock can lift a simple risotto from something quite ordinary to the sublime. Not everything freezes well, of course. I am not a fan of reheated frozen chicken, for example, unless it is in a pie. But to have a nourishing soup to heat up on a cold day, or a delectable spicy curry that only needs a fresh raita, or a homemade pie at the ready, takes the stress out of home cooking. I do bemoan the fact that I sometimes seem to be organising my life around a freezer, but such are the practicalities of feeding the hungry hordes. A frosty treasure chest of home-prepared meals – only requiring finishing fresh touches to restore life and spirit – delivers daily gifts.

80ml extra virgin olive oil

2 onions, peeled and diced

2 celery sticks, finely diced

6 garlic cloves, crushed

3 tablespoons tomato paste

2 teaspoons ground cumin

½ teaspoon ground coriander

½ teaspoon ground turmeric

½ teaspoon dried red chilli flakes

1kg white fish heads, trimmings and bones

2 x 400g tins chopped tomatoes

2 teaspoons sugar

to serve (per meal for 4)

about 30 clams (vongole), soaked in cold
   water to release sand

1 tablespoon lemon juice, or to taste

sea salt

freshly ground black pepper

pinch of sugar (optional)

1 tablespoon extra virgin olive oil

4 x 150g firm white fish fillets, such as
   snapper, ling, line-caught bass or
   organically farmed cod

chopped parsley

crusty bread

"If you are short on time, use a good quality fish stock in place of the water and omit the fish heads, trimmings and bones."

seafood soup

Heat the olive oil in a large cooking pot over a medium-high heat. Add the onions and celery, and cook, stirring occasionally, for about 5 minutes until translucent. Add the garlic, tomato paste, ground spices and chilli flakes, and cook, stirring, for a couple of minutes. Add the fish trimmings and bones, stir for a minute or two, then add the tomatoes, sugar and 1.5 litres water. Bring to the boil, lower the heat and simmer for 10 minutes. Allow to cool.

Strain the soup through a fine sieve, pushing down with the back of a wooden spoon to extract as much flavour from the fish and vegetables as possible. At this stage, you can freeze the soup base in two batches.

When ready to eat, gently reheat one batch of the frozen soup base in a saucepan over a low heat. Bring to the boil, then add the clams (vongole). Cover the pan tightly and simmer for a few minutes until the clams have opened. Add the lemon juice and season with salt, pepper and sugar to taste. Discard any unopened clams.

Heat the oil in a frying pan over a medium-high heat. Add the fish and fry skin side down for 2–3 minutes, then turn and cook for a further 1 minute.

To serve, divide the soup and clams between warm bowls and sprinkle over a little chopped parsley. Top each serving with a fish fillet. Accompany with crusty bread.

serves 4–6

1.5 litres freshly made chicken stock (see right)

1 leek, quartered lengthways and thinly sliced

6 celery sticks, diced

2 small turnips, diced

50g risoni pasta

150g peas (fresh or frozen)

250g shredded cooked chicken

sea salt

freshly ground black pepper

to serve

chopped flat-leaf parsley

freshly grated parmesan

crusty bread

chicken & vegetable soup
with risoni

Bring the chicken stock to the boil in a large saucepan over a high heat. Add the leek, celery and turnips, return to the boil, then lower the heat and simmer for 10 minutes.

If serving straight away, add the risoni and peas, if fresh, and simmer for a further 5 minutes until the risoni is al dente. If using frozen peas, add them a few minutes later as they will only take 2 minutes to cook. Add the shredded chicken and heat through. If freezing, add only the chicken, then cool and freeze at this stage.

To cook from frozen, reheat the soup until boiling. Add the risoni and peas, if fresh, and simmer for 5 minutes until the risoni is al dente and the peas are tender. If your peas are frozen, add them a few minutes later as they will only take 2 minutes to cook. Season with salt and pepper to taste.

Serve scattered with chopped parsley and grated parmesan, with crusty bread on the side.

chicken stock

Makes 2–3 litres

1 x 1.5kg chicken, rinsed, or 1.5kg chicken bones

2 onions, quartered

2 carrots, roughly chopped

2 celery sticks, roughly chopped

1 teaspoon black peppercorns

1 bay leaf

handful flat-leaf parsley

Place all the ingredients in a large saucepan with 4 litres cold water and slowly bring to the boil. Reduce the heat to very low and simmer gently for 2 hours. Skim off any scum or excess fat that rises to the surface. Strain the stock and leave to cool before refrigerating (for up to 4 days) or freezing. If you use a whole chicken, shred the meat and use for soup or sandwiches.

750g mixed greens, such as spinach,
 chard and sorrel, rinsed
8 spring onions, finely chopped
500g ricotta
125g feta, crumbled
80g parmesan, freshly grated
4 medium eggs, lightly beaten
small handful mint leaves, shredded
2 teaspoons sugar
1 teaspoon sea salt
freshly ground black pepper
3 tablespoons olive oil, or olive oil spray
16 sheets filo pastry (at least 20 x 30cm)
1 egg yolk, lightly beaten, to glaze

"I like to brush the filo pastry with olive oil, instead of the usual butter; an olive oil spray speeds up the process."

cheese & mixed greens filo pie

To make the pie filling, put the greens into a large frying pan or saucepan, cover with a tight-fitting lid and wilt over a high heat for a few minutes, until they have collapsed down. Tip into a colander and drain well. Roughly chop the greens and place in a large bowl. Add the spring onions, ricotta, feta, parmesan, eggs, mint, sugar, salt and pepper. Stir to combine.

Lightly oil a 20 x 30cm baking tin or foil baking dish and trim the filo sheets to the size of the tin. Lay one sheet of filo in the tin, brush or spray with olive oil and layer with another sheet of filo. Continue this process until 8 sheets are layered up. Spread the filling evenly on top.

Lay a sheet of filo pastry over the filling, spray or brush with olive oil and top with another sheet of filo. Continue until the rest of the filo sheets are layered up and the top layer is sprayed or brushed with olive oil. Trim the edges with a sharp knife or kitchen scissors. Cut a diamond pattern over the surface of the pie through the top layers of pastry.

If freezing, cover and freeze at this stage. If serving straight away, brush with egg yolk and bake in a preheated oven at 180°C/Gas 4 for 45 minutes.

To cook from frozen, brush the pie with beaten egg yolk and cook in a preheated oven at 180°C/Gas 4 for 1 hour or until crisp and golden brown on top.

Serve the pie with a roasted red pepper and tomato salad, seasoned with salt and pepper and dressed with a little lemon juice and a drizzle of olive oil.

serves 4

1 tablespoon extra virgin olive oil

1 onion, finely chopped

1 large carrot, finely diced

1 teaspoon ground cumin

2 teaspoons paprika

1 tablespoon tomato paste

190g red lentils

1.5 litres chicken or vegetable stock

to serve

2 handfuls baby spinach leaves

lemon juice, to taste

½ teaspoon sugar

sea salt

freshly ground black pepper

red lentil soup

Heat the olive oil in a large saucepan over a medium heat. Add the onion and cook until soft, then add the carrot, spices and tomato paste. Cook, stirring, for 1 minute, then add the lentils and stock. Bring to the boil, reduce the heat and simmer for 25–30 minutes or until the lentils are cooked. If freezing, cool and freeze in a suitable container at this stage.

To reheat from frozen, put the soup into a saucepan over a low heat, cover and heat through gently, stirring occasionally, until the soup reaches simmering point.

To finish, stir through the spinach leaves, lemon juice and sugar, and season with salt and pepper to taste.

serves 4 (or 6 for lunch)

6 fresh lasagne sheets, halved
35g parmesan, freshly grated

filling

1.25kg peeled, deseeded pumpkin
1 large red onion, cut into thin wedges
2 tablespoons extra virgin olive oil
2 teaspoons thyme leaves
½ teaspoon dried chilli flakes
sea salt
freshly ground black pepper

cheese sauce

40g butter
3 tablespoons plain flour
750ml milk
1 bay leaf
240g ricotta

to serve

simple tomato sauce (see page 91)

"I am not a big fan of heavy béchamel sauce, so I set myself a mission to create a baked pasta that is lighter. The addition of ricotta does the trick – and is no less satisfying."

pumpkin cannelloni

Preheat the oven to 200°C/Gas 6. For the filling, cut the pumpkin into 3cm cubes and scatter on a large baking tray with the onion. Drizzle over the olive oil and sprinkle with the thyme, chilli, salt and pepper. Bake for 40 minutes or until golden brown, giving an occasional stir. Remove and set aside to cool slightly. Place in a large bowl and mash with a fork, retaining some texture.

To make the cheese sauce, heat the butter in a large saucepan over a medium heat. Add the flour and cook, stirring, for 2–3 minutes or until bubbling. Gradually whisk in the milk, then add the bay leaf and cook, stirring, until the sauce is thickened and smooth. Remove from the heat, add the ricotta and whisk until combined. Season with salt and pepper to taste.

Lightly butter a baking dish or foil dish that will hold 12 cannelloni snugly. Spoon 3 tablespoons of the pumpkin filling down the middle of each halved lasagne sheet and fold to enclose the filling. Spread a third of the cheese sauce in the prepared dish and place the cannelloni on top in a single layer. Pour the remaining sauce over the top and sprinkle with grated parmesan.

Cover and freeze at this stage. Or, if you are serving straight away, bake in a preheated oven at 180°C/Gas 4 for 35–40 minutes until golden and bubbling. Serve with tomato sauce.

To cook from frozen, place in a preheated oven at 160°C/Gas 3 for about 45 minutes until golden and heated through. Serve with tomato sauce.

serves 4

12 pieces veal shank, about 4cm thick

plain flour, to dust

sea salt

freshly ground black pepper

60ml extra virgin olive oil

60g butter

1 garlic clove, finely chopped

1 white onion, finely chopped

1 celery stick, finely chopped

250ml dry white wine

1 bay leaf

125ml veal or chicken stock (or more)

gremolata

2 tablespoons finely chopped flat-leaf
  parsley

1 tablespoon finely shredded lemon zest

1 garlic clove, crushed

to serve

baked saffron risotto (see page 201)

"This is a change from the usual tomato-based osso buco. Serving it with my baked saffron risotto (see page 201) is a lovely, lazy alternative to a traditional risotto Milanese."

osso buco

Dust each veal shank with flour seasoned with salt and pepper. Heat the olive oil in a heavy-based frying pan or wide pan. Add the veal shanks and cook, turning as necessary, for 10 minutes or until well browned; you may need to do this in two batches. Remove and set aside. Add the butter, garlic, onion and celery to the pan and cook over a low heat for about 5 minutes until soft.

Arrange the veal shanks in the pan in a single layer. Pour in the wine and add the bay leaf. Bring to the boil, then cover, reduce the heat to low and simmer for 15 minutes. Add the stock and simmer for a further 1½–2 hours or until the meat is very tender and you can cut it with a fork. Check the liquid occasionally during simmering and add more stock or water if necessary.

Transfer the veal shanks to a plate. Discard the bay leaf. Increase the heat under the pan and cook the sauce for 1–2 minutes until thickened. Season to taste and return the veal shanks to the sauce. Cool and freeze in a suitable container at this stage, or if serving straight away, prepare the gremolata and finish as described below.

To reheat after freezing, defrost in the fridge for the day, or overnight, then place in a covered casserole in a preheated oven at 160°C/Gas 3 for 20–30 minutes, or until heated through.

For the gremolata, stir the chopped parsley, lemon zest and garlic together in a bowl. Stir half of the gremolata through the osso buco. Serve sprinkled with the remaining gremolata and accompanied by the risotto.

serves 4

40g fresh white breadcrumbs

60ml milk

1 tablespoon extra virgin olive oil

1 onion, finely chopped

1 garlic clove, crushed

350g pork mince

350g veal mince

1 medium egg

2 tablespoons chopped parsley

1 tablespoon chopped oregano

sea salt

freshly ground black pepper

plain flour, to dust

tomato sauce

2 tablespoons extra virgin olive oil

2 garlic cloves, crushed

2 x 400g tins chopped tomatoes

250ml chicken stock

½ teaspoon sugar

to serve

400g dried spaghetti

chopped parsley

classic
spaghetti &
meatballs

Preheat the oven to 200°C/Gas 6. Line a large baking tray with baking paper. Put the breadcrumbs into a bowl, pour on the milk and leave until the milk is absorbed. Heat the olive oil in a frying pan over a medium heat. Add the onion and cook, stirring occasionally, for 5 minutes or until soft. Add the garlic and cook, stirring, for another minute. Set aside to cool.

Put the pork and veal mince into a large bowl, add the soaked breadcrumbs, onion mixture, egg, herbs and seasoning. With clean hands, mix until well combined. Now wet your hands with a little water to prevent sticking and form the mixture into meatballs, about 3cm in diameter. Dust with a little flour, place on the prepared baking tray and bake for 20 minutes or until light golden.

Meanwhile, to make the tomato sauce, heat the olive oil in a large frying pan over a medium heat, add the garlic and cook, stirring, for 1 minute. Add the tomatoes, stock and sugar. Bring to the boil, then reduce the heat and simmer for 15 minutes.

Freeze the tomato sauce and meatballs separately at this stage, once cooled. Or, if eating straight away, add the meatballs to the sauce, cover and simmer for a further 20 minutes, adding a little water if necessary.

To reheat after freezing, defrost the sauce and meatballs in the fridge for the day, or overnight, then heat through together in a saucepan over a medium heat for 20–25 minutes.

To serve, cook the spaghetti in boiling salted water until al dente. Lift the meatballs out of the sauce into a warm bowl. Drain the spaghetti and toss with the tomato sauce. Serve topped with the meatballs and scattered with chopped parsley.

serves 4

1kg shoulder of lamb, trimmed of excess fat

3 tablespoons extra virgin olive oil

2 onions, halved and thinly sliced

4 garlic cloves, finely chopped

1 tablespoon freshly grated root ginger

1 tablespoon ground cumin

1 tablespoon ground coriander

1 teaspoon ground turmeric

2 cinnamon sticks

1 green chilli, deseeded and finely chopped

500ml thick yoghurt

1 teaspoon sugar

1 crisp apple, such as Granny Smith, grated

sea salt

freshly ground black pepper

to serve

large handful spinach leaves

steamed couscous or basmati rice

"This is a traditional Anglo-Indian style curry, freshened up with grated apple and yoghurt, and cooked very slowly."

nostalgic lamb curry with yoghurt & apple

Preheat the oven to 160°C/Gas 3. Cut the lamb into cubes. Heat half the olive oil in a flameproof casserole over a high heat and brown the lamb in batches for about 2 minutes on each side, until well browned. Remove and set aside.

Reduce the heat to medium and add the remaining oil to the pan. Add the onions and cook for 5 minutes, stirring occasionally, until translucent. Add the garlic and ginger and cook for 1 minute, then stir in the cumin, coriander, turmeric, cinnamon and chilli. Cook for 2 minutes, stirring.

Return the lamb to the pan and add the yoghurt, sugar, apple and 500ml water. Stir to combine, then cover with the lid and cook in the oven for 2 hours, or until meltingly tender. Season with salt and pepper to taste.

Cool and freeze in a suitable container at this stage, or complete the curry by adding the spinach leaves and serving with couscous or rice.

To reheat after freezing, defrost in the fridge for the day, or overnight, then place in a covered casserole in a preheated oven at 160°C/Gas 3 for 20–30 minutes, or until the curry is heated through. Stir the spinach leaves through the curry and serve with steamed couscous or basmati rice.

serves 4–5

1.2kg blade steak, trimmed

2 teaspoons Chinese five-spice powder

60ml mild-flavoured oil, such as sunflower

2 onions, diced

2 tablespoons Massaman curry paste

400ml coconut milk

300ml beef stock

2 tablespoons tamarind pulp (or lime juice)

1 tablespoon fish sauce

1 tablespoon brown sugar

400g waxy potatoes, peeled and cut into
  chunks

1 large carrot, cut into rounds

2 tablespoons chopped roasted peanuts

to serve

chopped roasted peanuts

Thai basil leaves

steamed rice

beef massaman
curry

Cut the beef into 3–4cm dice and toss in the five-spice powder to coat. Heat two-thirds of the oil in a large heavy-based pan or wok over a medium heat. Brown the beef in batches, for 2–3 minutes or until lightly and evenly coloured. Set the beef aside in a bowl.

Return the pan to a medium heat and add the remaining oil. Add the onions and cook, stirring occasionally, for 5 minutes or until soft. Stir in the curry paste and cook, stirring, for 2 minutes or until fragrant. Add the coconut milk, beef stock, tamarind pulp, fish sauce and sugar, and bring to the boil. Return the beef to the pan, reduce the heat to low and simmer gently for 30 minutes.

Add the potatoes (or these can be added after freezing, which is my preference). Add the carrot and peanuts, and simmer gently for a further 30–40 minutes or until the beef and vegetables are tender. Cool and freeze in suitable containers at this stage. Or, if serving the curry straight away, garnish with extra peanuts and Thai basil leaves, and accompany with steamed rice.

To reheat after freezing, defrost in the fridge for the day or overnight, then tip into a large saucepan with the potatoes (unless they've been added before freezing). Place over a medium heat, stirring occasionally, for 20–25 minutes until heated through and the potatoes are tender. Garnish with extra peanuts and Thai basil leaves, and accompany with steamed rice.

10g dried porcini mushrooms
500g skinless chicken breast fillets
60g plain flour
½ teaspoon cayenne pepper
1 teaspoon salt
freshly ground black pepper
2 tablespoons extra virgin olive oil
25g butter
1 small onion, finely diced
2 garlic cloves, crushed
150g mushrooms, sliced
80ml white wine (or water)
125ml single cream
1 tablespoon chopped sage
300g ready-made butter puff pastry
  (in a block or 4 sheets)
2 egg yolks, lightly beaten, to glaze

to serve
green salad

"Bake in a muffin tin to make 9 delightful little pies – perfect for a picnic as they can travel in the tin. Allow 25 minutes in the oven."

chicken & mushroom pies

Soak the dried porcini in 250ml just-boiled water for 30 minutes. Cut the chicken into 2–3cm dice. Combine the flour, cayenne, salt and pepper in a bowl. Add the chicken and toss to coat, shaking off any excess. Heat the olive oil and butter in a large frying pan over a high heat. Add the chicken and stir-fry until lightly browned and sealed (not cooked through). Remove and set aside.

Add the onion, garlic and fresh mushrooms to the pan and cook over a medium heat for 5 minutes, or until the mushrooms are coloured. Add the wine and let bubble for 1 minute. Chop the porcini and add with their soaking liquid and the cream. Simmer gently for a further 5 minutes. Add the chicken and cook for another minute. Remove from the heat and let cool, then stir in the sage.

Roll out the pastry on a lightly floured surface until 4mm thick. Cut out 4 rounds large enough to line 4 pie tins, 9.5cm in diameter, and 4 smaller rounds for the pie lids. Line the tins with the larger pastry rounds and spoon in the filling. Brush the edges of the pastry cases with egg yolk. Place the pastry tops on the pies and press the edges together to seal, then crimp with a fork. Make a slit in the top of each pie using a sharp knife.

Pies can be made and refrigerated or frozen in advance to this stage. If cooking now, brush with egg yolk and bake in a preheated oven at 180°C/Gas 4 for 35 minutes, or until golden brown.

To cook after freezing, allow the pies to thaw in the fridge for several hours, or overnight, then brush with egg yolk and bake as above.

Serve with a green salad.

friends over

I love having friends over for a meal. It's one of my favourite times to cook, though it hasn't always been so – I used to get into a panic about getting everything perfect and just so. Maybe it's age, maybe it's that I am comfortable in my skin, but I take it easier nowadays when entertaining, mainly on myself. I do like to be organised, preparing a few things ahead if I can, or simply gathering everything together ready to throw in the oven. And I do take care, because a special meal – like any other meal – should be prepared with love, and should be beautiful. Most importantly, it should be more about the people you are cooking for, than yourself. There is a fine balance between showing off and making an effort. When the first guests arrive, if all is well, I switch from cook to host. My marker of success is sitting down with my first glass of champagne or wine – to share conversation and time with friends who, in truth, I don't see as often as I would like to. At this point, I promise myself to make it sooner next time... as friends are the spice of life.

serves 4

500g minced beef or lamb

1 small onion, grated

55g fresh white breadcrumbs

3 tablespoons chopped flat-leaf parsley

5 tablespoons chopped coriander leaves

1 medium egg, lightly beaten

1 teaspoon ground cumin

1 teaspoon sweet paprika

1 red chilli, deseeded and finely chopped

sea salt

freshly ground black pepper

3 tablespoons extra virgin olive oil

tomato and tamarind sauce

2 tablespoons extra virgin olive oil

1 Spanish onion, finely diced

2 garlic cloves, sliced

1 tablespoon freshly grated root ginger

2 teaspoons ground cumin

1 teaspoon ground turmeric

1 tablespoon tamarind pulp
 (or 2 tablespoons lime juice)

2 x 400g tins chopped tomatoes

1 teaspoon sugar

to serve

coriander leaves, to garnish

mint sambal (see right)

spinach raita (see right)

pilaf with currants & cashews (see right)

(illustrated on previous pages)

baked meatballs
with tomato &
tamarind sauce

Preheat the oven to 220°C/Gas 7. Combine the minced meat, onion, breadcrumbs, parsley, coriander, egg, cumin, paprika, chilli and plenty of salt and pepper in a large bowl. Mix gently with your hands, then wet your hands and shape the mixture into small balls. Toss the meatballs gently in the olive oil in a roasting tin and bake for 10–15 minutes.

Meanwhile, to prepare the sauce, heat the olive oil in a large heavy-based pan over a medium-low heat. Add the onion and cook, stirring occasionally, for 5 minutes, or until it is translucent. Add the garlic, ginger, cumin and turmeric, and cook, stirring, for 2 minutes or until fragrant. Add the tamarind pulp, tomatoes, sugar, 1 teaspoon salt and a grinding of pepper. Cook, stirring frequently, for 10 minutes.

Add the meatballs to the sauce and stir carefully to coat them, then simmer gently for 10 minutes. Scatter with coriander leaves and serve with the mint sambal, spinach raita and pilaf.

"This highly-flavoured Indian-inspired meal calls for lots of chutneys and pickles. And if you are lucky enough to live near an Indian restaurant or Asian food store, buy some Indian sweets to serve as a quick dessert. Otherwise try a simple mango coupe – of fresh mango, vanilla ice cream and crushed macadamia nuts.

mint sambal

large handful mint leaves
60g shallots, finely sliced
1 small green chilli, finely diced
2 tablespoons lime juice
1 teaspoon sea salt

Tear the mint leaves roughly and place in a bowl. Add the rest of the ingredients and mix together gently. Leave to rest for 20 minutes before serving.

spinach raita

250g spinach, washed and shredded
500ml yoghurt (I use low-fat)
2 garlic cloves, crushed
sea salt
freshly ground black pepper

Place the spinach in a pan over a medium heat. Cover and cook, stirring occasionally, for 5 minutes, until wilted. Drain and cool.

Whisk the yoghurt together with the garlic, salt and pepper in a bowl until smooth. Add the spinach and stir to combine. Refrigerate until required.

pilaf with currants & cashews

1 tablespoon mild-flavoured oil, such as sunflower
1 teaspoon butter
1 onion, finely sliced
1 teaspoon sea salt
500g basmati rice
2 pinches of saffron threads
30g currants
2 tablespoons chopped toasted cashew nuts

Place a large pan (with a tight-fitting lid) over a medium-high heat. Add the oil and butter, then the onion and salt, and cook for 5–10 minutes, or until the onion is lightly coloured. Add the rice and stir for 1 minute. Pour in 1 litre boiling water, add the saffron and currants, and bring to the boil, stirring. Cover, reduce the heat to low and cook for 10 minutes. Turn off the heat and leave the pilaf to stand, covered, for 10 minutes; do not lift the lid. Serve scattered with chopped cashew nuts.

serves 4–6

1kg boneless pork shoulder, trimmed

2 tablespoons pomegranate molasses

1 small onion, grated

1 teaspoon ground coriander

1 teaspoon sea salt

1 teaspoon caster sugar

mango chutney

2 mangoes, peeled

2 tablespoons extra virgin olive oil

1 teaspoon black mustard seeds

1½ tablespoons freshly grated root ginger

75g sugar

1 red chilli, chopped (deseeded for less heat
   if preferred)

1½ tablespoons lime juice

to serve

creamed corn (see right)

red onion, olive & parsley salad (see right)

(illustrated on previous pages)

glazed pork skewers & mango chutney

Cut the pork into 4cm cubes. Put the pomegranate molasses, 80ml water, the onion, ground coriander, salt and sugar into a shallow non-metallic bowl and stir until combined. Add the pork and stir to coat in the marinade. Cover and refrigerate for at least 2–3 hours, preferably overnight.

To make the mango chutney, cut the mango flesh away from the stone and dice. Heat the olive oil in a medium saucepan, add the mustard seeds and stir until they start to pop. Add the ginger and cook for 30 seconds. Stir in the diced mangoes, sugar, chilli and salt to taste. Cook over a medium heat, stirring occasionally, for about 15 minutes until syrupy. Add the lime juice, check the seasoning and set aside to cool.

Preheat a griddle or barbecue on high. Drain off the excess marinade from the pork, then thread the meat onto 12 metal skewers. Grill or barbecue for 2–3 minutes each side or until lightly charred and cooked to your liking.

Serve the pork skewers with the mango chutney, creamed corn, and red onion, olive & parsley salad.

"This is the ultimate summer barbecue menu. Serve with piles of freshly warmed flat breads and seared asparagus, topped with butter, a squeeze of lime juice and sea salt. The blueberry pie (on page 233) would be a fitting finale, or you could just serve bowls of cherries or peaches."

creamed corn

1 tablespoon extra virgin olive oil
20g butter
1 onion, finely chopped
2 garlic cloves, crushed
4 corn cobs, kernels stripped
250ml chicken stock
sea salt
freshly ground black pepper

Heat the olive oil and butter in a pan over a medium heat. Add the onion and sauté for several minutes until starting to colour. Add the garlic and corn kernels and continue to cook for about 5 minutes or until the corn starts to colour. Pour in the chicken stock and simmer for about 20 minutes until the corn is tender.

Transfer half of the corn mixture to a blender and purée until smooth, then return to the pan. Stir to combine with the whole kernels and season with salt and pepper to taste.

red onion, olive & parsley salad

2 small red onions
about 2 bunches flat-leaf parsley, leaves
  stripped
100g baby green olives
2 lemons
2 tablespoons extra virgin olive oil
sea salt
freshly ground black pepper

Cut the onions into very thin rounds, preferably with a mandolin. Place in a large bowl with the parsley leaves and olives, and toss to mix. Cut away the peel and white pith from the lemons, then cut the flesh into very thin slices and add to the salad. Drizzle with the olive oil, season with sea salt and pepper, and toss to combine.

serves 4

1 x 1.5kg chicken, rinsed and patted dry

marinade

4 garlic cloves, roughly chopped

1 red chilli, finely chopped (optional)

1 teaspoon coriander seeds

sea salt

125ml extra virgin olive oil

1 tablespoon sherry vinegar

2 tablespoons lime juice

2 tablespoons orange juice (freshly squeezed)

freshly ground black pepper

to serve

salbitxada sauce (see right)

couscous, pea & olive salad (see right)

barbecued chicken & salbitxada sauce

Remove the backbone from the chicken by cutting either side of the bone. Flatten out with the palm of your hand, then slash the chicken in a few places on each side. Place in a dish, cover and set aside in the fridge.

For the marinade, pound the garlic, chilli, coriander seeds and 1 teaspoon salt to a paste, using a pestle and mortar. Transfer to a bowl. Heat the olive oil in a small pan, then pour over the paste. Add the sherry vinegar, lime and orange juices and whisk to combine. Season with pepper. Pour half of the marinade over the chicken and marinate in the fridge for an hour. (Save the rest for your next barbecue.)

Heat a barbecue (with lid) to high with the lid down. Place the chicken cut-side down on the rack, close the lid and cook for 30 minutes, until the chicken is cooked through. (Or cook, skin side up on a baking tray, in a preheated oven at 220°C/Gas 7 for 30–35 minutes until cooked through.)

Serve the barbecued chicken with the salbitxada sauce and couscous, pea & olive salad.

"This jewel-coloured al fresco meal is full of Spanish flavours. The marinade is a brilliant all-rounder for all kinds of meat and fish, and keeps well in the fridge. Make extra if you are feeding a crowd and marinate some lamb and fresh chorizo to make your chicken go further. Finish off with a silky caramel custard (see page 222)."

salbitxada sauce

3 ripe tomatoes
1 roasted red pepper, peeled and diced
30g blanched almonds, toasted and
  roughly chopped
½ teaspoon dried chilli flakes
½ teaspoon paprika
3 garlic cloves, crushed
1 teaspoon finely grated lemon zest
2 tablespoons chopped flat-leaf parsley
  leaves
1 tablespoon sherry vinegar
125ml extra virgin olive oil
sea salt
freshly ground black pepper

Halve, core, deseed and finely dice the tomatoes. Place in a bowl and add the red pepper, almonds, chilli flakes, paprika, garlic, lemon zest, parsley and sherry vinegar. Heat the olive oil in a small pan, then pour over the tomato mix and stir to combine. (Or pulse the ingredients in a food processor, retaining a chunky texture.) Season with salt and pepper to taste. The sauce can be prepared ahead and kept in the fridge for a couple of days.

couscous, pea & olive salad

225g couscous
375ml chicken stock
pinch of saffron threads
150g peas (blanched fresh or thawed frozen)
1 red pepper, cored, deseeded and diced
100g green olives, pitted and chopped
2 tablespoons extra virgin olive oil
1 tablespoon lemon juice
1 tablespoon orange juice
1 tablespoon sherry vinegar
sea salt
freshly ground black pepper
2 handfuls flat-leaf parsley, chopped

Put the couscous into a large heatproof bowl. Bring the stock and saffron to the boil in a pan, pour over the couscous, cover and let stand for 5 minutes. Fluff up with a fork and stir through the peas, red pepper and olives.

For the dressing, whisk together the olive oil, lemon and orange juices, sherry vinegar, salt and pepper in a bowl. Pour over the couscous salad, toss to mix and leave to stand for 20–30 minutes. Stir through the parsley.

serves 4

4 tablespoons cornflour

2 tablespoons sea salt

2 teaspoons freshly ground white pepper (or
  you could use black)

20 large raw prawns, peeled and
  deveined (tails intact if preferred)

about 1 litre mild-flavoured oil, such as
  sunflower, for deep-frying

to serve

1 red chilli, deseeded and sliced

lemon wedges

(illustrated on previous pages)

salt & pepper prawns

Put the cornflour, salt and pepper in a medium bowl and stir to combine. Add the prawns and toss to dust with the seasoned cornflour mixture. Shake off the excess and set aside on a tray. (Don't leave them sitting for long like this or they will get soggy and won't be as crunchy and delicious as they should be.)

Meanwhile, heat the oil in a wok to 190°C, or until a cube of bread dropped in browns in less than a minute. Fry the prawns in batches, trying not to crowd the wok, for around 2 minutes until they are just opaque. Remove with a slotted spoon and drain on kitchen paper. Once the prawns are all cooked, deep-fry the sliced chilli in the oil for 1–2 minutes. Remove with a slotted spoon and drain on kitchen paper.

Arrange the prawns on a warm serving platter, top with the fried chilli and serve immediately, with lemon wedges on the side.

serves 4

4 duck leg quarters

2 tablespoons soy sauce

1 tablespoon Chinese rice wine,
  or dry sherry

1 tablespoon sesame oil

2 tablespoons hoisin sauce

to serve

shredded spring onions

steamed rice

steamed greens with soy dressing (see right)

tomato salad with spring onion & sesame
  oil (see right)

(illustrated on previous pages)

glazed duck

Preheat the oven to 160°C/Gas 3. Place the duck quarters on a baking tray. Combine the soy, rice wine and sesame oil in a small bowl. Brush the duck with the mixture and roast for 1¼ hours, brushing occasionally with more of the soy mix.

Combine a small amount of the soy mix with the hoisin sauce to thin it and brush over the duck. Return to the oven for a further 20 minutes or until dark golden.

Serve the glazed duck garnished with spring onions and accompanied by steamed rice and the other components of your Chinese meal.

"This range of textures, ingredients and cooking styles provides a balanced Chinese meal, and the luxury ingredients say special occasion. Finish with the gooey chocolate cake with raspberries (on page 230) if it's a birthday celebration, or chilled watermelon slices for a lighter, refreshing dessert."

seasonal greens with soy dressing

500g seasonal green vegetables, such as
  pak choi, gai lan, mangetout, sugar
  snap peas, asparagus

soy dressing
80ml soy sauce
2 tablespoons Chinese black vinegar (or
  balsamic vinegar)
1 tablespoon mild-flavoured oil, such as
  sunflower
1 chilli, finely chopped (deseeded for less
  heat if preferred)
1 teaspoon sugar
1 tablespoon lime juice

First make the soy dressing: put all of the ingredients into a bowl and stir well to combine.

Blanch the green vegetables in boiling salted water until tender yet crisp and bright green. Drain and arrange on a warm serving plate. Pour over the dressing and serve.

tomato salad with spring onion & sesame oil

4 tomatoes, chopped
2 spring onions, finely chopped
1 teaspoon sesame oil
1 red chilli, finely chopped (deseeded for less
  heat if preferred)
1 teaspoon sea salt

Put the tomatoes into a bowl and mash lightly with a fork to release the juices. Add the rest of the ingredients, toss to combine and let sit for 5 minutes before serving.

serves 4

1 tablespoon extra virgin olive oil

1 teaspoon sea salt

4 x 180g salmon fillets, with skin

minted peas

2 tablespoons extra virgin olive oil

1 onion, chopped

1 garlic clove, crushed

250ml chicken stock

500g frozen peas

1 teaspoon sugar

large handful mint leaves, chopped

to serve

cucumber & yoghurt salad (see right)

sweet potato cakes (see right)

lemon wedges

(illustrated on previous pages)

baked salmon

Preheat the oven to 140°C/Gas 1. Drizzle the olive oil over the bottom of a small baking dish and sprinkle evenly with salt. Lay the salmon fillets skin side down in the dish and bake for 15 minutes until just cooked through; the salmon will have a 'glassy' appearance.

Meanwhile, for the minted peas, heat the olive oil in a saucepan, add the onion and sauté until just starting to colour. Add the garlic, chicken stock, peas and sugar, and cook gently for 15 minutes. Mash with a fork or potato masher, add the mint leaves and season with salt and pepper to taste.

Serve the salmon and minted peas with the cucumber & yoghurt salad, sweet potato cakes and lemon wedges.

"For a vegetarian meal, omit the salmon and replace with a salad of Puy lentils, chopped celery and blanched green beans dressed in red wine vinegar and a little olive oil. Complete the meal with a strawberry vacherin (see page 221)."

cucumber & yoghurt salad

1 Lebanese (short) cucumber
250ml thick Greek yoghurt
2 tablespoons chopped flat-leaf parsley
1 tablespoon lemon juice
sea salt
freshly ground black pepper

Halve the cucumber lengthways, scoop out the seeds and finely dice the flesh. Place in a bowl with the yoghurt, parsley and lemon juice. Toss to mix and season with salt and pepper to taste.

sweet potato cakes

500g sweet potatoes, peeled
60g plain flour
1 teaspoon baking powder
1 tablespoon curry powder
1 tablespoon brown sugar
sea salt
freshly ground black pepper
2 red chillies, deseeded and finely chopped
3 spring onions, finely sliced
handful coriander leaves, finely chopped
2 medium eggs, lightly beaten
60ml milk
sunflower oil, for shallow-frying

Grate the sweet potatoes coarsely. Mix the flour, baking powder, curry powder, sugar, salt, pepper, chillies, onions and coriander together in a bowl. Add the eggs and enough milk to make a stiff batter. Stir in the grated potatoes. Cook in batches: heat a 1cm depth of oil in a deep frying pan until almost smoking. Drop in a few tablespoonfuls of batter and flatten. Fry over a medium-high heat for several minutes on each side until golden. Drain on kitchen paper. Keep warm in a low oven while you cook the rest, then serve.

serves 4

4 veal loin chops (or use pork loin chops)
2 tablespoons extra virgin olive oil
sea salt
freshly ground black pepper
2 garlic cloves, finely sliced
1 anchovy fillet, finely chopped
125ml white wine
250g cherry tomatoes
1 tablespoon marjoram leaves

to serve
baked saffron risotto (see right)
fennel & rocket salad

(illustrated on previous pages)

veal chops
with tomato
& marjoram

crostini with ricotta & salsa verde

8 thin slices good quality bread, such as sourdough
extra virgin olive oil, for drizzling
sea salt
freshly ground black pepper
100g ricotta

salsa verde

2 large handfuls flat-leaf parsley, finely shredded
4 red or green spring onions, finely chopped
4 tablespoons extra virgin olive oil
3 tablespoons lemon juice
3 good quality anchovy fillets in oil (tinned or in jars),
  finely chopped
1 tablespoon salted capers, rinsed, dried and chopped

Preheat the oven to 180°C/Gas 4. For the salsa verde, stir
all the ingredients together in a bowl to combine and
season with pepper only, to taste. The texture should be
quite coarse. Transfer to a serving dish.

Cut each slice of bread in half on the diagonal and lay on a
baking tray. Drizzle with olive oil and season with salt and
pepper. Bake until golden brown, about 12 minutes. Put
the ricotta in a bowl, drizzle with a little olive oil and season.

Put the toast on a warm platter. Let everyone assemble
their own crostini, topping the toasted bread with ricotta
and a dollop of salsa verde.

"Have the crostini as a nibble with a glass of Prosecco or Campari and soda before sitting down to dinner. Try flavouring the veal with another herb, such as rosemary, thyme or sage, and add a crunchy salad of finely sliced fennel and rocket dressed in a little lemon juice, olive oil and sea salt. Round off the meal with a tempting tiramisu ice cream cake (see page 226)."

Brush the veal with 1 tablespoon olive oil and season liberally with salt and pepper. Heat a large frying pan over a high heat. When hot, add the veal chops and cook for 1–2 minutes on each side until golden. Transfer to a plate and set aside.

Add the remaining olive oil, garlic and anchovy to the pan and stir over the heat for 30 seconds. Pour in the white wine and let bubble for 1 minute to reduce, scraping the bottom of the pan with a spatula to deglaze.

Add the cherry tomatoes and cook until they begin to blister, then return the veal chops to the pan and cook for 5 minutes, turning them once. Stir the marjoram through and serve, with the baked saffron risotto and fennel & rocket salad.

1 tablespoon extra virgin olive oil
15g butter
1 onion, finely chopped
1 teaspoon sea salt
pinch of saffron threads
180g arborio rice
625ml beef or chicken stock

Preheat the oven to 200°C/Gas 6. Heat a large ovenproof dish (with a lid) over a medium-high heat. Add the olive oil, butter, onion, salt and saffron, and cook, stirring, for 5 minutes, or until the onion is soft and translucent.

Add the rice to the dish and stir over the heat for another minute. Add the stock and bring to the boil. Cover and bake in the oven for 30 minutes, or until the rice is cooked al dente.

serves 4

4 tablespoons extra virgin olive oil

1 x 1.5kg farmed free-range rabbit, jointed

2 chorizo sausages, diced

1 onion, roughly chopped

3 garlic cloves, thinly sliced

1 red pepper, cored, deseeded and diced

2 celery sticks, sliced

1 leek, trimmed and sliced

2 bay leaves

3 thyme sprigs

3 green chillies, deseeded and finely chopped

1 teaspoon sweet paprika

400g tin chopped tomatoes

200ml sherry or white wine

sea salt

freshly ground black pepper

to serve

2 tablespoons chopped flat-leaf parsley

olive oil mash (see right)

green beans with shallots (see right)

rabbit with chorizo
& green chilli

Heat the olive oil in a large casserole or deep frying pan over a medium heat. Add the rabbit pieces and chorizo and cook for 10 minutes, turning to colour evenly on all sides. Remove from the pan and set aside.

Add the onion, garlic and red pepper to the same pan and cook for 5 minutes. Add the celery, leek, bay leaves and thyme, and cook for a further 5 minutes. Add the chillies and paprika and stir to combine.

Return the rabbit and chorizo to the pan, and add the tomatoes and sherry. Cover and cook for about 30 minutes until the rabbit pieces are cooked through. Season with salt and pepper to taste.

Scatter over the chopped parsley and serve immediately, with the mash and green beans.

"Once viewed as a cheap alternative to the luxury of chicken, rabbit is now considered more of a gourmet treat. If you find it hard to come by, however, you can always substitute chicken pieces. This is a wonderful, hearty meal for the cooler months – follow with the lemon posset (on page 223) for a light, tangy conclusion."

olive oil mash

1kg floury potatoes, such as King Edward,
  peeled
3 garlic cloves, peeled
250ml milk
50g unsalted butter, diced
50ml extra virgin olive oil
sea salt
freshly ground black pepper

Cut the potatoes into chunks and cook in a pan of boiling salted water with the garlic until tender. Meanwhile, slowly heat the milk in another pan, removing it from the heat just before it comes to the boil.

Drain the potatoes and garlic, return to the pan and mash. Add the hot milk, stirring constantly with a wooden spoon, to make the mash light and fluffy. Add the butter and continue stirring, then incorporate the olive oil and season with salt and pepper to taste. Serve immediately.

green beans with shallots

250g green beans, topped and tailed
1 tablespoon extra virgin olive oil
25g unsalted butter
1 garlic clove, finely chopped
1½ shallots, finely chopped
2 teaspoons finely chopped flat-leaf parsley
sea salt
freshly ground black pepper

Blanch the beans in a saucepan of lightly salted boiling water for 2–3 minutes until bright green and tender yet crisp. Rinse under cold running water and drain well.

Heat the olive oil and butter in a frying pan over a medium heat. Add the garlic and shallots and fry for 30 seconds. Add the beans and sauté for 1½ minutes. Add the chopped parsley, season with salt and pepper to taste and serve.

makes 36

175g tinned chickpeas, drained
200g long-grain rice
250g tinned chopped tomatoes
2 red onions, finely diced
1½ teaspoons ground cumin
1 teaspoon paprika
1 red chilli, finely diced
2 tablespoons mint leaves, finely chopped
small handful flat-leaf parsley leaves, chopped
sea salt
freshly ground black pepper
200g vine leaves in brine, rinsed and drained
1 tablespoon lemon juice

garlic yoghurt

2 garlic cloves
¼ teaspoon sea salt
250ml yoghurt

to serve

extra virgin olive oil
lemon wedges

(illustrated on previous pages)

"You can make this mezze-style menu easier by buying the dolmades, some dips and olives. For meat-eaters, add some barbecued spiced sausages or chicken wings marinated in lemon juice and garlic. For a delightful finish, serve the strawberry vacherin (on page 221), or buy some Turkish delight or baklava."

dolmades
with garlic yoghurt

For the garlic yoghurt, crush the garlic with the salt and mix with the yoghurt. Cover and leave for 1 hour to allow the flavours to combine.

To make the filling for the dolmades, place the chickpeas, rice, tomatoes, onions, cumin, paprika, chilli, mint, parsley, salt and pepper in a bowl and stir well to combine.

To make the dolmades, take a vine leaf, making sure it is not broken, and place one tablespoon of filling in the centre. Roll up the vine leaf halfway, fold in the edges and then roll up completely. Continue until all of the filling is used.

Line a deep frying pan (with lid) with the leftover vine leaves. Place the dolmades in the frying pan, in tightly packed rows. Pour the lemon juice and 250ml water over them and add a little salt. Cover the pan and bring to the boil. Reduce the heat to medium and cook for 40–50 minutes, checking from time to time that the pan isn't drying out and adding a little more water if necessary.

Using a slotted spoon, lift the dolmades onto a warm platter and drizzle with a little olive oil. Serve with lemon wedges and the garlic yoghurt dip, as part of a selection of mezze dishes (see right).

1 cauliflower, about 600g, cut into florets

3 medium eggs, separated

sea salt

freshly ground black pepper

80g plain flour

1 onion, finely grated

3 garlic cloves, crushed

1 teaspoon ground cumin

1 teaspoon ground coriander

¼ teaspoon ground turmeric

handful flat-leaf parsley leaves, chopped

125ml olive oil, for shallow-frying

to serve

handful flat-leaf parsley leaves, chopped

lemon wedges (optional)

225g burghul

2 tablespoons extra virgin olive oil, plus
  extra for drizzling

1 onion, finely chopped

100g pimentos (in jar), drained and finely
  sliced

small handful flat-leaf parsley leaves, finely
  chopped, plus extra to serve

40g chopped walnuts, plus extra to serve

1 pomegranate, seeds extracted (optional)

1 tablespoon pomegranate molasses

2 tablespoons lemon juice

1 teaspoon paprika

1 teaspoon ground coriander

sea salt

freshly ground black pepper

cauliflower fritters

Blanch the cauliflower florets in boiling salted water for 1–2 minutes. Drain and refresh under cold water.

To make the batter, lightly whisk the egg yolks in a bowl. Add 1 teaspoon salt and some pepper. Gradually add the flour, alternately with 200ml water, whisking continuously. Stir through the onion, garlic, spices and parsley. In another bowl, whisk the egg whites until soft peaks form. Fold half the egg whites through the batter mixture using a metal spoon, then fold in the rest.

Cook the fritters in batches: heat the olive oil in a deep frying pan over a medium-high heat until smoking. Dip the cauliflower florets into the batter to coat, allowing excess to drip off, then carefully drop into the hot oil, being careful not to overcrowd the pan. Fry, turning occasionally, for 2–3 minutes, until the cauliflower florets are browned all over. Remove and drain on kitchen paper. Keep warm while you cook the rest.

To serve, arrange the fritters on a warm platter, season with salt and pepper and garnish with parsley. Serve with lemon wedges for squeezing, if you like.

burghul, pimento & paprika salad

Place the burghul in a bowl, pour over enough cold water to cover and leave to stand for 20–30 minutes.

Meanwhile, heat the olive oil in a frying pan over a medium-high heat. Add the onion and cook, stirring occasionally, until translucent. Remove from the heat and allow to cool.

Squeeze out excess water from the burghul with your hands and place in a large bowl. Add the onion, pimentos, parsley, walnuts, pomegranate seeds, pomegranate molasses, lemon juice, paprika, coriander, salt and pepper, and stir to combine.

Pile the salad onto a serving platter and scatter with extra chopped walnuts and parsley to serve.

serves 4–6

1.7kg leg of lamb, trimmed of excess fat
4 garlic cloves, crushed
1 tablespoon chopped rosemary leaves
extra virgin olive oil, for drizzling
sea salt
freshly ground black pepper
4 good quality anchovy fillets in oil (tinned or in jars)
500ml chicken stock
1 tablespoon tomato paste
1 tablespoon balsamic vinegar
2 tablespoons finely grated orange zest
juice of 1 orange
60g pitted black olives

to serve

potato gratin (see right)
tomato confit (see right)

(illustrated on previous pages)

roast leg of lamb
with anchovies & orange

Rub the lamb all over with garlic and rosemary, drizzle with olive oil and season with salt and pepper. If possible, leave to marinate in a cool place for a couple of hours, or overnight in the fridge if time permits.

Preheat the oven to 200°C/Gas 6. Place the lamb in a roasting tray and roast for 1½ hours, or until cooked to your liking.

Transfer the lamb to a warm platter and set aside to rest in a warm place. Put the roasting tin over a medium heat, add the anchovies and break them up with a wooden spoon, then pour in the stock, stirring to deglaze. Add the tomato paste and balsamic vinegar and stir until slightly reduced. Add the orange zest and juice. Stir until reduced and slightly thickened, then add the olives.

Slice the lamb and serve with the sauce, potato gratin and tomato confit.

"To simplify this dish, omit the potato gratin and tomato confit. Instead, toss quartered, peeled potatoes in olive oil and throw them into the roasting tray with the lamb, then serve the roast with a tomato salad. Finish with an apricot upside down tart (see page 225) or a gooey chocolate cake with raspberries (see page 230)."

potato gratin

25g butter
1 tablespoon extra virgin olive oil
3 large onions, halved and thinly sliced
1 teaspoon thyme leaves
1.2kg yellow waxy potatoes, such as
    Charlotte or Nicola, peeled if preferred
30–40g butter
750ml chicken stock
sea salt
freshly ground black pepper

Preheat the oven to 200°C/Gas 6. Heat a frying pan over a medium heat and add the butter and olive oil. When the butter has melted, fry the onions, stirring, for 10 minutes until golden brown. Stir through the thyme.

Peel and slice the potatoes very finely, using a mandoline, if you have one. Arrange a third of the potatoes in a medium baking dish, scatter over a third of the onions, dot with butter and season well. Repeat the layers twice, finishing with an onion layer. Pour over the chicken stock, cover with foil and bake for 40 minutes. Uncover and cook for a further 20 minutes or until the top is golden brown and the potatoes feel tender when tested with a knife.

tomato confit

1kg ripe plum tomatoes
4 garlic cloves, lightly crushed with a knife
2 thyme sprigs
125ml extra virgin olive oil
sea salt
small handful basil leaves
freshly ground black pepper

Preheat the oven to 150°C/Gas 2. Quarter the tomatoes lengthways and cut out the core and seeds, leaving just the flesh attached to the skin. Drizzle some of the olive oil onto a baking tray and place the tomatoes cut side up on the tray. Scatter over the garlic cloves and thyme sprigs, drizzle over the remaining olive oil and season liberally with salt. Bake for 30 minutes, then turn the tomatoes and cook for a further 30 minutes.

Remove from the oven and allow to cool on a tray. The tomatoes can be kept in a sealed container in the fridge for a couple of days, but make sure you bring them to room temperature before eating. Slip off the skins and serve the confit tomatoes scattered with basil leaves and sprinkled with pepper.

sweet dreams

For most of us these days, specially prepared desserts tend to be reserved for entertaining, rather than a daily occurrence. However, recently, after incessant demands from my children, I came up with a **midweek dessert night**. Naively, I thought it would soon be forgotten, but no, like movie night, it is here to stay and my repertoire of **easy desserts** has grown remarkably. A luscious caramel sauce can be made in minutes and is delectable poured over good quality vanilla ice cream, while perfectly ripe fruit is **nature's ultimate dessert**. Who can resist a fragrant mango, figs drizzled with a little honey, raspberries eaten straight from the punnet, or juicy cherries that you just can't eat enough of before their season disappears? When I have enough time, I'll **bake a pudding** or prepare something **more elaborate**. I have come to enjoy dessert night – the air of anticipation and delight it brings. And a longer, lingering meal topped off with the **luxury of a sweet treat** is the perfect send-off to dreamy bliss.

serves 4

160g caster sugar

1 teaspoon vanilla bean paste or vanilla extract

2 cinnamon sticks

6 medium firm, ripe pears (about 200g each)

coffee sauce

95g soft brown sugar

250ml double cream

1 teaspoon natural vanilla extract

15g butter

1 shot of espresso (or 30ml very strong black
  coffee)

to serve

vanilla ice cream

"This is a dessert that can be prepared up to two days before serving – a winner for midweek entertaining. Poach your pears and make the caramel sauce ahead, but warm both before serving."

poached pears
with warm
coffee sauce

Heat 1 litre water with the sugar, vanilla and cinnamon in a large saucepan, stirring to dissolve the sugar. Bring to the boil, reduce the heat to medium and simmer for 5 minutes. In the meantime, peel and core the pears, leaving the stalk intact, and cut a thin slice off the bottom so they can stand upright. Add the pears to the pan and bring to a simmer. Poach gently, turning occasionally, for 10–15 minutes or until tender.

Meanwhile, place all the ingredients for the sauce in a small saucepan over a medium heat, stir to combine and bring to a slow boil. Cook, stirring occasionally, for 5 minutes or until thick and syrupy.

Remove the pears from the syrup with a slotted spoon. Serve them drizzled with the warm coffee sauce and a scoop of vanilla ice cream.

250g ripe, best quality strawberries
250g caster sugar
4 medium egg whites
pinch of sea salt

to serve
vanilla or strawberry ice cream

"If you can get hold of excellent quality strawberry ice cream, this is the time to use it."

strawberry vacherin

Preheat the oven to 120°C/Gas ½. Line a baking tray with baking paper. In a bowl, crush 4 or 5 ripe strawberries with 1 tablespoon sugar, using the back of a fork.

Place the egg whites and salt in a clean, dry, large bowl and whisk until soft peaks form. Add the rest of the sugar gradually, whisking continuously, until the mixture becomes stiff and glossy. Add the crushed strawberry mixture gradually and whisk through.

Spoon the meringue into 8 mounds on the prepared baking tray and bake for 1¼ hours. Remove from the oven and allow to cool. (The meringues can be stored in an airtight container for up to a week.)

To serve, top each meringue with a scoop of ice cream and scatter with the rest of the strawberries.

serves 8–10

170g caster sugar

375g tinned sweetened condensed milk

5 medium eggs

1 litre milk

1 teaspoon natural vanilla extract

½ teaspoon ground cinnamon

silky caramel custard
with cinnamon

Preheat the oven to 180°C/Gas 4. Have ready a 23cm round ovenproof ceramic dish (or cake tin), about 5cm deep.

To make the caramel, put the sugar into a small heavy-based saucepan and melt over a medium heat. Cook to a deep golden caramel, stirring occasionally with a fork, then immediately pour into the ceramic dish and tilt to coat the bottom. Be very careful as the caramel is extremely hot and it will make the dish hot too.

Let the caramel cool completely, for about 10–15 minutes, then stand the dish on a folded tea towel in a roasting tray large enough to hold it comfortably (this will be your bain-marie).

For the custard, whisk the condensed milk and eggs together in a large bowl to combine, then whisk in the milk, vanilla and cinnamon. Pour the mixture through a fine strainer into the caramel-lined dish. Cover the dish with foil, then pour enough boiling water into the roasting tray to come halfway up the side of the dish.

Carefully place in the oven and bake for 1 hour, or until the custard is just set but still wobbly. Remove the dish from the bain marie. Allow to cool, then chill in the fridge for at least 4 hours, or overnight.

To invert, run a sharp knife around the edge of the custard, place an upturned serving dish on top and invert both. Lift off the baking dish and serve the custard immediately.

serves 8

180ml lemon juice (about 4 lemons)

125g caster sugar

500ml double cream

to serve

slivered unsalted pistachio nuts or berries

lemon posset

Strain the lemon juice into a medium saucepan, add the sugar and stir over a low heat until the sugar has dissolved. Take off the heat.

Meanwhile, pour the cream into another small saucepan and bring to the boil. Whisk the cream into the sweetened lemon juice until combined. Pour into 8 shot glasses and chill until set, about 3 hours.

Serve sprinkled with a few slivered pistachio nuts, or some berries.

"When I did a TV show with the English dessert chef, Claire Clark, from the French Laundry in the Napa Valley, I was bowled over by the simplicity of her lemon posset, which inspired this recipe. Claire serves her posset with shortbread."

serves 4-6

100g butter

12 apricots, halved and pitted (or
  1kg apricots tinned in juice)

90g soft light brown sugar

1 teaspoon natural vanilla extract

125g plain flour

2 teaspoons baking powder

1 teaspoon ground cinnamon

115g caster sugar

130ml soured cream

to serve

crème fraîche or whipped cream

"It is important to turn the tart out immediately, so that the apricots don't set and stick to the pan."

apricot upside down tart

Preheat the oven to 200°C/Gas 6. Cut 75g of the butter into small pieces and set aside. If using tinned apricots, drain well and pat dry with kitchen paper.

In a 24cm ovenproof frying pan, melt the remaining 25g butter together with the brown sugar and vanilla. Cook for 1 minute, stirring to dissolve the sugar. Remove from the heat and arrange the apricots, cut side down, in the pan.

Sift the flour, baking powder and cinnamon together into a bowl and stir in the caster sugar. Add the butter pieces and rub in with the fingertips until the mixture resembles breadcrumbs. Add the soured cream, stirring to combine. Spoon the mixture over the apricots and bake for 30 minutes until golden.

As you remove the tart from the oven, immediately invert it carefully onto a serving platter. Cut into slices and serve topped with a dollop of crème fraîche or whipped cream.

serves 8

125ml strong black coffee, cooled

60ml Kahlua (or other coffee liqueur)

60ml Marsala

200g savoiardi (sponge finger biscuits)

1.5 litres vanilla ice cream, softened

150g good quality dark chocolate, grated

tiramisu
ice cream
cake

Line a 20cm square baking tin with baking paper. Combine the coffee, Kahlua and Marsala in a bowl.

One at a time, briefly dip half of the savoiardi into the coffee mix and use to line the base of the tin. Layer half of the ice cream on top and then sprinkle with half of the grated chocolate. Repeat these layers, then place in the freezer for 4 hours or until frozen.

About 30 minutes before you will be ready to eat the tiramisu, transfer to the fridge to soften. Carefully lift it out of the tin onto a plate, using the baking paper. Cut into squares to serve.

"This is one of those impressive desserts that really is a bit of a cheat. Just make sure that you let it sit in the fridge while you're having dinner – to soften enough for the ice cream to be luscious and the cake easy to cut."

"The beauty of this cake is that it virtually self-ices. It also works terrifically well with apricot jam."

topping

100g good quality dark chocolate

150g raspberry jam

125ml single cream

cake

30g good quality cocoa powder

60ml milk

½ teaspoon natural vanilla extract

90g raspberry jam

115g butter, softened

65g caster sugar

2 medium eggs

125g plain flour

1½ teaspoons baking powder

pinch of sea salt

80g raspberries, plus extra
  to serve

(illustrated on previous pages)

gooey chocolate cake
with raspberries

Preheat the oven to 180°C/Gas 4. Generously grease a 22cm round cake tin. For the topping, put the chocolate, jam and cream into a small pan over a medium heat. Stir until smooth, then pour into the prepared tin.

In a bowl, mix the cocoa powder with 125ml boiling water, stirring until smooth, then add the milk, vanilla and jam, whisking to combine.

In a large bowl, cream the butter and sugar together until light and fluffy, then add the eggs one at a time, mixing well after each. Sift the flour, baking powder and salt into a separate bowl. Using a large spoon, fold the dry ingredients and the cocoa mix into the creamed mixture, alternating the two, then fold the raspberries through.

Pour the mixture into the cake tin, ensuring you spread it right to the edge and cover the topping completely. Bake for 30–35 minutes or until firm. Leave the cake to cool in the tin for 15 minutes. (If not serving straight away you can refrigerate the cake in the tin, but you will need to warm it in the oven before turning it out.)

Turn the cake out onto a plate. You may need to scrape some sauce out of the tin and spread it over the top of the cake. Serve warm or cold, with fresh raspberries.

serves 4

125g plain flour

3 teaspoons baking powder

1 teaspoon ground cinnamon

115g caster sugar

200g peeled and cored pineapple, cut into
  1cm dice

250ml milk

85g unsalted butter, melted and cooled

1 medium egg, lightly beaten

135g soft light brown sugar

3 tablespoons golden syrup

to serve

pouring custard (see right), ice cream
  or single cream

pineapple layer pudding

Preheat the oven to 180°C/Gas 4. Sift the flour, baking powder and cinnamon into a bowl and stir in the caster sugar. Add the diced pineapple, milk, melted butter and egg, and mix well until evenly combined. Turn the mixture into a 2 litre baking dish, about 7cm deep.

Put the brown sugar, golden syrup and 250ml water into a small saucepan and heat slowly until the sugar dissolves. Bring to the boil, then take off the heat and pour evenly over the surface of the pudding. Bake for 30–40 minutes until puffed and golden.

Beneath the light sponge topping, you will find a caramel sauce layer as you cut into the pudding. Serve with custard, ice cream or single cream.

pouring custard

4 medium egg yolks

500ml milk

55g caster sugar

1 teaspoon natural vanilla extract

Put the egg yolks into a small heavy-based saucepan. Heat the milk, sugar and vanilla in another small saucepan until just scalded. Gradually pour the mixture onto the egg yolks, stirring constantly with a wooden spoon.

Cook over a medium heat, stirring continuously, until the custard thickens enough to thinly coat the back of the spoon; don't let it boil or it may curdle. Immediately remove from the heat.

serves 6–8

pastry

500g plain flour

60g icing sugar

pinch of sea salt

360g unsalted butter, chilled and cubed

130ml soured cream

filling

500g blueberries (fresh or frozen)

115g caster sugar

1 teaspoon finely grated lemon zest

1 tablespoon lemon juice

2 tablespoons cornflour

2 medium egg yolks, lightly beaten

2 tablespoons white or demerara sugar,
  to sprinkle

to serve

pouring custard (see page 231),
  or single cream

"This is one of the most rewarding things to make. The buttery soured cream pastry contrasts perfectly with the sweet tartness of the blueberries – superb with pouring custard, or with single cream."

blueberry pie

To make the pastry, sift the flour, icing sugar and salt into a bowl. Add the butter and rub in with your fingertips until the mixture resembles coarse breadcrumbs. Add the soured cream and mix until the dough comes together in a ball. (Alternatively, put the sifted flour, icing sugar and salt into a food processor and pulse a few times to combine. Add the butter and pulse until the mixture resembles coarse breadcrumbs, then add the soured cream and pulse until a dough ball forms.) Divide the dough in half, shape into balls and wrap each one in plastic wrap. Refrigerate for 30 minutes before using.

Preheat the oven to 200°C/Gas 6. Unwrap one pastry ball and roll out on a lightly floured surface to a 4mm thick round. Use to line a 23cm pie tin, lightly pressing the pastry into the corners, then trim the edge. Roll out the other pastry ball to a similar round and place on a board. Place the pie tin in the freezer for at least 15 minutes. Cover the other pastry sheet with plastic wrap and place in the fridge.

For the filling, toss the blueberries with the caster sugar, lemon zest, lemon juice and cornflour. Scatter evenly in the pastry case. Brush the rim of the pastry case with egg yolk, then lay the pastry round on top to cover the pie. Trim and press the pastry edges firmly together to seal, then crimp the rim with a fork dipped in flour.

Brush the top with egg yolk, sprinkle with sugar and make 5 small incisions in the pie lid. Stand the pie tin on a baking tray and bake for 15 minutes, then reduce the heat to 170°C/Gas 3 and bake for a further 35 minutes or until golden.

Allow the pie to cool before serving, with pouring custard or cream.

serves 4–6

1kg plums

125g plum jam

2 tablespoons honey

2 teaspoons lemon juice

2 cinnamon sticks

1 tablespoon caster sugar

rice pudding

2 medium eggs

100g caster sugar

1 teaspoon natural vanilla extract

800ml milk

2 tablespoons arborio or short-grain rice

to serve

freshly grated nutmeg

single cream

baked plums
with rice pudding

Preheat the oven to 140°C/Gas 1. Halve and stone the plums and place, cut side up, in a shallow ovenproof dish in a single layer. Combine the plum jam, honey, lemon juice and 250ml water in a saucepan and stir over a medium heat until melted and combined. Pour over the fruit, add the cinnamon sticks and sprinkle with the caster sugar.

For the rice pudding, whisk the eggs, sugar and vanilla extract together in a bowl. Whisk in the milk, then stir though the rice. Pour into a 1 litre ovenproof dish. Stand the dish in a larger baking tray and pour enough hot water (from the kettle) into the tray to come halfway up the sides of the dish.

Bake the rice pudding in the middle of the oven, with the plums on the shelf above, for 1 hour, or until just set and lightly golden on top; it should still be wobbly. Take the pudding out of the oven, turn up the setting to 220°C/Gas 7 and bake the plums for a further 10 minutes.

Meanwhile, take the rice pudding dish out of the water bath and set aside to rest for 10 minutes. Grate some nutmeg over the top and serve, with the warm baked plums and single cream.

index

For Natalie, Edie, Inès and Bunny

I would like to take this opportunity to thank Alison Cathie, for her faith in me and my recipes, Rick McKenna for his guidance, experience and strength, Helen for her beautiful creative direction, John Kernick for his inspired and delicious photography, Susie for her energy, passion and opinions, Rebecca and Fern for consistent output of picture-perfect food, Jane O'Shea for steering the boat, Janet for her patience, kindness and careful editing, the team at Quadrille who will coddle and feed this book on its journey, and Grace and Diana for their tenacity while testing, even in the face of food science challenges. An extra special thanks to the team at bills who keep the dream alive by working so hard and loyally, thank you, thank you, thank you. A huge thank you also to Old Granny Patsy, without whose love and care of the girls this book would not have been what it is, to Edie, Inès and Bunny for their open palates and being harsh critics – "I won't be dreaming about this dinner, Daddy!" – and Natalie, whose love makes everything possible.

First published in 2009 by
Quadrille Publishing Limited
Alhambra House, 27–31 Charing Cross Road,
London WC2H 0LS
www.quadrille.co.uk
Text © 2009 Bill Granger
Photography © 2009 John Kernick
Design and layout © 2009 Quadrille Publishing Limited

Cataloguing in Publication Data: a catalogue record for this book is available from the British Library.

ISBN 978 184400 706 6

Printed in Spain

Publishing director Jane O'Shea
Creative director Helen Lewis
Project editor Janet Illsley
Photographer John Kernick
Food and props stylist Susie Theodorou,
   assisted by Rebecca Jurkevich and Fern Green
Fashion stylist Simon Willis
Assistant designer Nicola Davidson
Production Vincent Smith, Ruth Deary

The publisher would also like to thank the following for the loan of bowls and plates for photography: BrickettDavda www.brickettdavda.com and Daniel Smith handmade plates, available from Eskandar.com